FROM
DAWN TO DAWN

TROUBADOUR POETRY

Translated into English from the Occitan by

A. S. KLINE

POETRY IN TRANSLATION
www.poetryintranslation.com

Please direct sales or editorial enquiries to:
tonykline@poetryintranslation.com

This print edition is published by
Poetry In Translation (*www.poetryintranslation.com*),
via On-Demand Publishing LLC, (a Delaware limited liability Company that does
business under the name "CreateSpace") in partnership with
Amazon Services UK Limited(a UK limited company with registration number
03223028 and its registered office at 1 Principal Place, Worship Street, London,
EC2A 2FA)

ISBN-10: 1722867019
ISBN-13: 978-1722867010

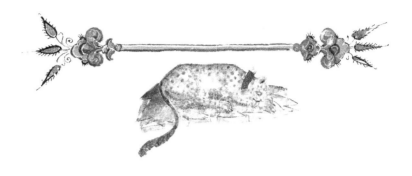

'Per solatz revelhar,
Que s'es trop enformitz,
E per pretz, qu'es faiditz
Acolhir e tornar,
Me cudei trebalhar'

'To wake delight once more
That's been too long asleep,
And worth that's exiled deep
To gather and restore:
These thoughts I've laboured for'

Guiraut de Bornelh

'Musician playing a viol'
John of Abbeville, Sermones dominicales
Last quarter of the 13th century or
first quarter of the 14th century

CONTENTS

Translator's Introduction

he troubadour tradition of lyric poetry originated in eleventh century Occitania – a region comprising what is now southern France together with portions of Catalonia and northern Italy. Occitania, whilst a cultural union linguistically founded on the Occitan language, was neither a legal nor political entity in its own right. The troubadour school of Occitan poetical and musical fiction, rich in genre and satire, concerned itself principally with the twin themes of chivalry and courtly love. Spreading across Europe over two and a half centuries, the tradition eventually waned in popularity and died out around the time of the Black Death.

This personal selection of Occitan poetry is of verse that I feel has true poetic merit, and nothing is included solely for its historic interest. I considered a simple prose or free verse translation of these poems, but to show the Troubadours without their rhyme schemes, their form, seemed to me too great an admission of failure. Form is half their art and crucially their poems were set to music, a large amount of which survives.

Either approach, rhymed or un-rhymed, is of course valid. As always the end result is what counts. I have gone for rhyme *and* aimed for accuracy of meaning. These translations attempt to stay close to the original text, in rhythm, rhyme-scheme and content. I have given the first lines of the poems, the *incipits*, as Occitan headings (one only is in Latin).

Many dates and facts are conjecture, and so the order of the poets is at times somewhat arbitrary where dates of birth and death are uncertain. I have not translated the *vidas*, or biographical lives of the poets, which are highly unreliable, though charming as legend, but have referred to them where relevant.

ANONYMOUS (10TH CENTURY)

he manuscript of this bilingual text, which has been termed the first *alba* or dawn song, made of Latin stanzas with an apparently Provençal refrain, is thought to have come from the monastery of Fleury-sur-Loire. Though not strictly a troubadour text, it is a first example of a form, the *alba*, adopted later. The refrain is: *L'alb' apar, tumet mar at ra'sol; po y pas, a! bigil, mira clar tenebras!*

PHEBI CLARO NONDUM ORTO IUBARE

With pale Phoebus, in the clear east, not yet bright,
Aurora sheds, on earth, ethereal light:
While the watchman, to the idle, cries: 'Arise!'

Dawn now breaks; sunlight rakes the swollen seas;
Ah, alas! It is he! See there, the shadows pass!

Behold, the heedless, torpid, yearn to try
And block the insidious entry, there they lie,
Whom the herald summons urging them to rise.

Dawn now breaks; sunlight rakes the swollen seas;
Ah, alas! It is he! See there, the shadows pass!

From Arcturus, the North Wind soon separates.

The star about the Pole conceals its bright rays.

Towards the east the Plough its brief journey makes.

Dawn now breaks; sunlight rakes the swollen seas;

Now, alas! It is he!

Note: *The third verse suggests a summer sky in northern latitudes, say late July, when Arcturus sets in the north-west at dawn.*

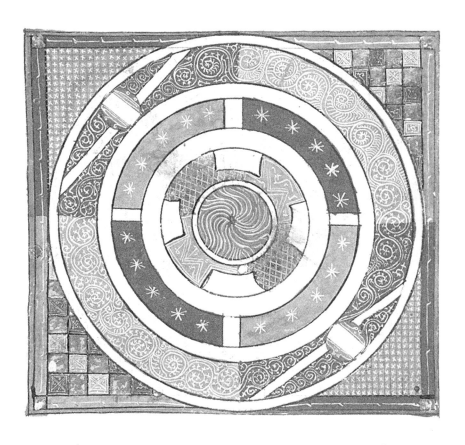

'Miniature of a diagram of the sun with rays'
Breviari d'amor, Matfres Eymengau de Beziers, first half of
the 14th century

GUILLAUME DE POITIERS (1071 - 1127)

illiam or Guillem IX, called The Troubador, was Duke of Aquitaine and Gascony and Count of Poitou, as William VII, between 1086, when he was aged only fifteen, and his death. Refusing to take part in the first crusade of 1098, he was one of the leaders of the minor Crusade of 1101 which was a military failure. He was the 'first' troubadour, that is, the first recorded vernacular lyric poet, in the Occitan language. Threatened with excommunication several times for his dissolute life and challenges to Church authority, he was later reconciled. He married his 'step-daughter' Anor, to his son, later Guilhem X, and in turn their daughter Alianor (Eleanor), Duchess of Aquitaine and Countess of Poitou, became Queen of France, and by her second marriage to Henry, Duke of Normandy, later Henry II, became Queen of England also. She was the mother of the Young King Henry, Richard Coeur de Lion, Geoffrey of Brittany and John Lackland.

AB LA DOLCHOR DEL TEMPS NOVEL

Out of the sweetness of the spring,
The branches leaf, the small birds sing,
Each one chanting in its own speech,
Forming the verse of its new song,
Then is it good a man should reach
For that for which he most does long.

From finest sweetest place I see
No messenger, no word for me,
So my heart can't laugh or rest,
And I don't dare try my hand,
Until I know, and can attest,
That all things are as I demand.

This love of ours it seems to be
Like a twig on a hawthorn tree
That on the tree trembles there
All night, in rain and frost it grieves,
Till morning, when the rays appear
Among the branches and the leaves.

So the memory of that dawn to me
When we ended our hostility,
And a most precious gift she gave,
Her loving friendship and her ring:
Let me live long enough, I pray,
Beneath her cloak my hand to bring.

I've no fear that tongues too free
Might part me from Sweet Company,
I know with words how they can stray
In gossip, yet that's a fact of life:
No matter if others boast of love,
We have the loaf, we have the knife!

Note: *Pound quotes the phrase* 'Ab la dolchor' *at the start of Canto XCI.*

'Garden of pleasures'
Guillaume de Lorris and Jean de Meung
Roman de la Rose, c. 1400

FARAI UN VERS DE DREYT NIEN

I've made a song devoid of sense:
It's not of me or other men
Of love or being young again,
Or other course,
Rather in sleep I found it when
Astride my horse.

I know not what hour I was born:
I'm not happy nor yet forlorn,
I'm no stranger yet not well-worn,
Powerless I,
Who was by fairies left one morn,
On some hill high.

I can't tell whether I'm awake
Or I'm asleep, unless men say.
It almost makes my poor heart break
With every sigh:
Not worth a mouse though, my heart-ache,
Saint Martial, fie!

I'm ill, I'm afraid of dying;
But of what I hear know nothing;
I'd call a doctor for his learning,
But which, say I?
He's a good doctor if I'm improving,
Not, if I die.

I've a lover, but who is she?
She, by my faith, I never could see;
Nothing she did to hurt or please,
So what, say I?
In my house, no French or Norman
Shall ever lie.

I never saw her, yet love her true,
She never was faithful or untrue;
I do well when she's not in view,
Not worth a cry,
I know a nobler, fairer too
To any eye.

I've made the verse, don't know for who;
I'll send it on to someone new,
Who'll send it on towards Anjou,
Or somewhere nigh,
So its counter-key from his casket he'll
Send, by and by.

Note: *The last two lines remain perplexing, but suggest that Guillaume was inviting a similarly ironic song, a counter or duplicate, in reply.*

'Medical consultations'
Roger Frugardi of Salerno, Chirurgia
First quarter of the 14th century

PUS VEZEM DE NOVELH FLORIR

Since we see, fresh flowers blowing
Field and meadow greenly glowing,
Stream and fountain crystal flowing
Fair wind and breeze,
It's right each man should live bestowing
Joy as he please.

Of love I'll speak nothing but good.
Why've I not had all that I could?
Likely I've had all that I should;
For readily,
It grants joy to one who's understood
Love's boundary.

It's been the same all of my days,
I've had no joy of love, always,
Too late now to change my ways;
For knowingly
I've done much of which my heart says:
'That's nullity.'

For this reason I win less pleasure:
What I can't have I always treasure;
And yet the saying proves true forever:
For certainly:
'To good heart comes good luck in measure' –
Suffer joyfully!

You will never prove faithful to
Love, unless you're submissive too,
And to neighbours and strangers you
Act quite humbly,
And to all who live within its view
Obediently.

Obedience we must ever show,
To others, if we'd love, and so
It's fitting that from us should flow
True courtesy;
We must not speak at court as though
Born vilely.

This verse I'll say to you is worth
More if you'll comprehend it first,
And praise the words, I gave them birth
Consistently,
I too will praise, as finest on earth,
Its melody.

My Stephen, though here I keep my berth,

There presently,

I trust you'll read this, and of its worth

Give guarantee.

MOUT JAUZENS ME PRENC EN AMAR

Great the joy that I take in love,
A joy where I can take my ease,
And then in joy turn as I please,
Once more with the best I move,
For I am honoured, she's above
The best that man can hear or see.

I, as you know, small credit take,
Nor for myself claim any power,
Yet if ever a joy should flower,
This one should, and overtake
All others, Earth from shadows wake
Like the sun in a gloomy hour.

No man can fashion such a thing,
By no wish of his, no desire,
Nor by thought or dream aspire
To such joy, as she will bring,
All year I could her praises sing
And not tell all before I tire.

All joys are humbled, all must dance
To her law, and all lords obey
My lady, with her lovely way
Of greeting, her sweet pleasant glance,
A hundred years of life I'd grant
To him who has her love in play.

Her joy can make the sick man well,
And through her anger too he dies,
And fools she fashions of the wise,
And handsome men age at her spell,
And status, wealth she can dispel
And raise the beggar to the skies.

Since man can find no better here,
That lips can tell of, eyes can see,
I wish to keep her close by me.
To render my heart fresh and clear,
Renew the flesh too, so the sere
Winds of age blow invisibly.

If she'll grant her love in measure,
My gratitude I'll then declare,
And conceal it and flatter there,
Speak and act all for her pleasure;
Carefully I'll prize my treasure,
And sing her praises everywhere.

I daren't send this by another,
I have such fear of her disdain,
Nor go myself, and go in vain,
Nor forcefully make love to her;
Yet she must know I am better
Since she heals my wound again.

'Philosophy'
Boethius (anonymous French translation)
Le Livre de Boece de Consolacion (Book 4), 1477

FARAI CHANSONETA NUEVA

I'll make a little song that's new,
Before wind, frost, and rain come too;
My lady tests me, and would prove
How, and in just what way, I am
In love, yet despite all she may do
I'd rather be stuck here in this jam.

I'd rather deliver myself and render
Whatever will write me in her charter,
No, don't think I'm under the weather,
If in love with my fine lady I am,
Since it seems I can't live without her,
So great the hunger of sire for dam.

For she is whiter than ivory,
So there can be no other for me.
If there's no help for this, and swiftly,
And my fine lady love me, goddamn,
I'll die, by the head of Saint Gregory,
If she'll not kiss me, wherever I am!

What good will it be to you, sweet lady,
If your love keeps you distant from me?
Are you hankering after a nunnery?
Know this then: so in love I am,
I'm fearful lest pure sadness claim me,
If you don't right my wrongs, madam.

What good if I seek a monastery,
And you don't keep tight hold of me?
All the joy of the world we'd see,
Lady if we were ewe and ram.
To my friend Daurostre, I make this plea,
That he sing (not bray) this at my command:

For her I shiver and tremble,
Since with her I so in love am;
Never did any her resemble,
In beauty, since Eve knew Adam.

'Eve'
Giovanni Boccaccio, De Claris Mulieribus, c. 1440

POS DE CHANTAR M'ES PRES TALENTZ

Since my mood urges me to sing
I'll make a verse, of my grieving:
Yet not serve Love in anything,
In Poitou or in Limousin.

Now to exile I have come:
In great fear and danger's room,
And fierce war I'll leave my son,
By his neighbours ill is planned.

This parting now makes me rue
The Seigneury of Poitou!
Fulk of Angers keeps it true,
With his kin, all the land.

If Fulk fails these lands to succour,
And the king, from whom's my honour,
Then that crew will bring dishonour
Gascon felons and Angevin.

If neither good nor worth he knows,
When I'm gone from you, suppose
They'll quickly cause his overthrow
Knowing him young: but half a man.

Mercy I ask of each companion,
If I have wronged him may he pardon;
And I ask it of Jesus in heaven
Both in Latin and Romance.

I was of joy and chivalry,
But now of both I must be free;
And to Him I now take me,
Where sinner finds his goal at hand.

Happiness, gaiety have I seen
But our Lord bans what has been;
Will not suffer such ill scenes,
When so near my end I stand.

All have I left for love of Him,
Chivalry and pride grow dim;
And if God please, he'll gather me in,
And I pray keep me at his right hand.

I ask that my friends at my death
Come but to honour my last breath,
For I have had both joy and mirth
Near and far, and in palace grand.

So, I abandon joy and mirth,
Vair, sable, ermine: I'll naked stand.

Note: *Fulk is Foulques V of Anjou (its capital Angers) also known as Foulques the Younger, Count of Anjou 1109-1129, and King of Jerusalem from 1131 to his death in 1143*

'Funeral Service'
Book of Hours, Use of Rouen, c. 1485 - c. 1495

JAUFRE RUDEL (D. C. 1148)

he Castellan of Blaye, he flourished early to mid 12th century and probably died during the Second Crusade, 1147-9. His 13th century *vida* or biography claims he fell in love with the Countess of Tripoli without ever having seen her and after taking ship for Tripoli fell ill during the voyage, ultimately dying in the arms of his 'love afar'.

LANQUAN LI JORN SON LONC E MAY

When the days are long, in May,
Sweet the songs of birds afar,
And when I choose from there to stray,
I bring to mind a love that's far.
I walk face lowered, and I glower,
And neither song nor hawthorn flower,
Can please me more than winter's ice.

I hold the Lord for truth always
By whom was formed this love afar,
But for each good that comes my way
Two ills I find, since she's so far.
Would I were a pilgrim at this hour,
So staff and cloak from her tower,
She'd gaze on with her lovely eyes!

What joy it will be to seek that day,
For love of God, that inn afar,
And, if she wishes, rest, I say,
Near her, though I come from afar,
For words fall in a pleasant shower
When distant lover has the power,
With gentle heart, joy to realise.

Sad, in pain, would I go away,
Should I not see that love afar.
For I don't know when I may
See her, the distance is so far.
So many the roads and ways lower,
That indeed I can say no more,
But let all things be as she likes.

The delights of love I never may
Enjoy, if not joy of my love afar,
No finer, nobler comes my way,
From any quarter: near or far.
So rich and high is her dower,
That there in the Saracen's tower
For her sake I would be their prize.

God that made all that goes or stays
And formed this love from afar
Grant me the power to hope one day
I'll see this love of mine afar,
Truly, and in a pleasant hour,
So that her chamber and her bower,
Might seem a palace to my eyes.

Who calls me covetous, truth to say,
Is right, I long for a love afar,
For no other joy pleases me today
Like the joy in my love from afar.
Yet what I wish is not in my power,
It is my godfather's curse, so sour,
That I love, yet love should be denied.

For what I wish is not in my power,
Cursed my godfather's word so sour,
Who has ruled my love should be denied.

QUAN LO RIUS DE LA FONTANA

When the sweet fountain's stream
Runs clear, as it used to do,
And there the wild-roses blow,
And the nightingale, on the bough,
Turns and polishes, and makes gleam
His sweet song, and refines its flow,
It's time I polished mine, it would seem.

Oh my love, from a land afar,
My whole heart aches for you;
No cure can I find, for this no
Help but your call, I vow,
With love's pangs sweetest by far,
In a curtained room or meadow,
Where I and the loved companion are.

I shall lack that forever though,
So no wonder at my hunger now;
For never did Christian lady seem
Fairer – nor would God wish her to –
Nor Jewess nor Saracen below.
With manna he's fed as if in dream,
Who of her love should win a gleam!

No end to desire will my heart know
For her, whom I love most, I vow;
I fear lest my will should cheat me,
If lust were to steal her from me too.
For sharper than thorns this pain and woe
The sadness that joy heals swiftly,
For which I want no man's pity.

Without parchment brief, I bestow
On Filhol the verses I sing now,
In the plain Romance tongue, that he
May take them to Uc le Brun, anew.
They rejoice in it, I'm pleased to know,
In Poitou, and in Berry,
In Guyenne, and Brittany.

Note: *Uc le Brun is Uc VII of Lusignan, who had taken the cross for the Second Crusade in 1147. Filhol is the name of the* joglar (jongleur, *or minstrel)*

NO SAP CHANTER QUI SO NO DI

No one can sing where no melody is,
Or fashion verse with words unclear,
Or know how the rhymes should appear,
If his logic inwardly goes amiss;
But my own song begins like this:
My song gets better, the more you hear.

Let no man wonder about me,
If I love one I've never known,
My heart joys in one love alone,
That of one who'll never know me;
No greater joy do I welcome gladly,
Yet I know not what good it may be.

I am struck by a joy that kills me,
And pangs of love that so ravish
All my flesh, body will perish;
Never before did I so fiercely
Suffer like this, and so languish,
Which is scarce fitting or seemly.

How often do I close my eyes
And know my spirit is fled afar;
Never such sadness that my heart
Is far from where my lover lies;
Yet when the clouds of morning part,
How swiftly all my pleasure flies.

I know I've never had joy of her,
Never will she have joy of me,
Nor promise herself, nor will she
Ever now take me as her lover;
No truth or lie does she utter,
To me: and so it may ever be.

The verse is good, I have not failed,
All that is in it is well placed;
He whose lips it may chance to grace,
Take care it's not hacked or curtailed
When Bertran in Quercy's assailed,
Or, at Toulouse, the Count you face.

The verse is good, and they'll be hailed
For something they'll do in that place.

MARCABRU (FL. 1130 - 1150)

arcabru was a powerful influence on later poets who adopted the *trobar clus* style. He experimented, as here, with the *pastorela*. Among his patrons were William X of Aquitaine and, probably, Alfonso VII of León. Marcabru may have travelled to Spain in the entourage of Alfonso Jordan, Count of Toulouse, in the 1130s. In the 1140s he was a propagandist for the *Reconquista*, of Spain from the Moors.

A LA FONTANA DEL VERGIER

In an orchard down by the stream,
Where at the edge the grass is green,
In the shade of an apple-tree,
By a plot of flowers all white,
Where spring sang its melody,
I met alone without company
One who wishes not my solace.

She was a young girl, beautiful,
Child of the lord of that castle;
But when I thought the songbirds' call
Might, from its tree, make her heart light,
And sweet the fresh season all,
And she might hear my prayers fall,
A different look did cross her face.

Her tears flowed, the fount beside,
And from her heart her prayer sighed.
'Jesus, King of the World,' she cried,
'Through you my grief is at its height,
Insult to you confounds me, I
Lose the best of this world wide:
He goes to serve and win your grace.

With you goes my handsome friend,
The gentle, noble, and brave I send;
Into great sorrow I must descend,
Endless longing, and tears so bright.
Ai! King Louis to ill did tend
Who gave the order and command,
That brought such grief to my heart's space!'

When I heard her so, complaining,
I went to her, by fountain's flowing:
'Lady,' I said 'with too much crying
Your face will lose its colour quite;
And you've no reason yet for sighing,
For he who makes the birds to sing,
Will grant you joy enough apace.'

'My lord,' she said, 'I do believe
That God will have mercy on me
In another world eternally,
And many other sinners delight;
But here he takes the thing from me
That is my joy; small joy I see
Now that he's gone so far away.'

CERCAMON (FL. C. 1137 - 1152)

orn apparently in Gascony, his real name unknown, he probably spent most of his career in the courts of William X of Aquitaine and Eble III of Ventadorn. He was the inventor of the *planh*, the Provençal dirge, and some circumstantial evidence points to his having died on crusade as a follower of Louis VII of France.

QUANT L'AURA DOUSSA S'AMARZIS

When the sweet air turns bitter,
And leaves fall from the branch,
And birds their singing alter
Still I, of him, sigh and chant,
Amor, who keeps me closely bound,
He that I never had in my power.

Alas! I gained nothing from Amor
But only had pain and torment,
For nothing is as hard to conquer
As that on which my desire is bent!
No greater longing have I found,
Than for that which I'll lack ever.

In a jewel I rejoice, in her
So fine, no other's felt my intent!
When I'm with her I dumbly stutter,
Cannot utter my words well meant,
And when we part I seem drowned,
Loss of all sense and reason suffer.

All the ladies a man saw ever
Compared to her aren't worth a franc!
When on earth the shadows gather,
Where she rests, all is brilliant.
Pray God I'll soon with her be wound,
Or watch her as she mounts the stair.

I startle and I shake and shiver
Awake, asleep, on Love intent,
So afraid that I might wrong her,
I don't dare ask for what I meant,
But two or three years' service downed,
Then she'll know the truth I offer.

I live nor die, nor am made better
Nor feel my sickness though intense,
Since with her Love I want no other,
Nor know if I'll have it or when,
For in her mercy does all abound,
That can destroy me or deliver.

It pleases me when she makes me madder,
Makes me muse, or in gaping rent!
It's fine if she plays the scorner
Laughs in my face, or at fingers' end,
For, after the bad, the good will sound,
And swiftly, should that be her pleasure.

If she wants me not, I'd rather
I'd died the day my service commenced!
Ah, alas! So sweet she did murder
Me, when she gave her Love's assent,
And tied me with such knots around,
That I desire to see no other.

All anxiously I delight in her,
For whether I fear or court her then
Is up to her; or be false or truer,
Trick her, or prove all innocent,
Or courteous or vile be found,
Or in torment, or take my leisure.

But, who it may please or who astound,
She may, if she wants, retain me there.

Say I: scarce courteous is he crowned,
The man who shall of Love despair.

'Christine de Pisan presenting her book
to queen Isabeau of Bavaria'
Christine de Pizan, Various works
(also known as 'The Book of the Queen')
c. 1410 - c. 1414

RIGAUT DE BERBEZILH (FL. 1140 - 1163)

igaut, also Richart or Richartz, de Berbezilh, also Berbezill or Barbesiu, French: *Rigaud de Barbezieux*, Latin: *Rigaudus de Berbezillo*, was of the petty nobility of Saintonge. He was a major influence on the Sicilian School and is quoted in the *Roman de la Rose*. The *Planh* below was previously attributed, by Pound and others, to Bertran de Born.

SI TUIT LI DOL E·LH PLOR E·LH MARRIMEN

If all the grief and woe and bitterness
The pain, the harm and all the misery
Yet heard of in this grievous century
Were set together, they would seem but light
Against the death of the young English king.
He leaves worth clouded, and youth dolorous,
The world obscure, shadowed and in darkness,
Void of all joy, full of despair and sadness.

In pain and sadness, full of bitterness
Are left behind the courteous soldiery,
The troubadours, the subtle minstrelsy,
In Death they find a foe of greater might,
Who's taken from them the young English king,
That made the freest hand seem covetous.
There are no more, nor were in past excess
Of this world, the tears to drown such sadness.

Relentless Death, so full of bitterness,
Well may you boast now the most knightly
Chevalier you have taken, best of any,
For there is nothing worthy of delight
That belonged not to this young English king;
If it pleased God, it were better for us
That he should live than many of the rest
Who offer us no joy but grief and sadness.

From this pale world, so full of bitterness
Love flies, his deceits must be taken lightly,
Nothing is his indeed but pains us swiftly;
And less than yesterday is each day's light.
All saw themselves in this young English king
Who of the world was the most virtuous;
Gone is his body, amorous in finesse,
Leaving us pain, and discord, and great sadness.

He whom it pleased in all our bitterness

To come to earth to raise us from misery,

And died His death, to bring us victory,

Him do we ask, of mercy, Lord of right

And of humility, that the young English king

He please to pardon, if pardon be for us,

And with honoured companions grant him rest,

There where there is no grief, nor any sadness.

Note: *The young English king was the charismatic Henry Plantagenet (1155-1183) an elder brother to Richard Coeur de Lion, and twice crowned king in his father Henry II's lifetime, a Capetian custom. He predeceased his father, and so never wielded power, dying of dysentery while on campaign in the Limousin.*

BERNART DE VENTADORN (FL. 1145 - 1175)

ccording to the troubadour Uc de Saint Circ, Bernart was the son of a baker at the castle of Ventadour or Ventadorn, in the Corrèze. His first patron was Viscount Eble III of Ventadorn. He composed his first poems for his patron's wife, Marguerite de Turenne. Uc de Saint Circ has him ultimately withdrawing to the Cistercian abbey of Dalon and dying there.

'Like to the lark ascending, in the air, first singing and then silent, content with the final sweetness that sates her'

*— Dante:*Paradiso XX:*73-75*

CAN VEI LA LAUZETA MOVER

When I see the lark display
His wings with joy against the day,
Forgetting, fold then fall away,
As sweetness to his heart makes way,
Such great envy then invades
My mind: I see the rest take fire,
And marvel at it, for no way
Can my heart turn from its desire.

Ah, I so dearly wished to know
Of love, yet so little learn,
For I cannot keep from loving her
Who will not have me, though I burn.
She stole my heart, and all of me,
And she herself, and worlds apart;
Lacking herself, now nothing's left
But longing and the willing heart.

For 'I' has no power over 'I'
Nor has had since the day I know
I let myself gaze in her eye,
The mirror that pleased me so.
Mirror, now I'm mirrored in you,
Profound sighs are killing me,
I lost myself as he did too
Narcissus gazing in the deep.

Of every lady I despair!
And in them I can place no trust!
Those I once would seek to cheer
Leave them cheerless now I must.
Seeing her then who won't have me,
She who destroys me and confounds,
I doubt them all and can't believe,
Knowing them other than they're found.

My lady shows herself, not to my good,
A woman indeed, scorns my behest,
Since she wishes not what she should
But what's forbidden her finds best.
Now I'm fallen from all grace,
I've done well on the asses' bridge!
And don't know why I'm in disgrace,
Except I've asked a world too much.

Mercy's lost, and gone from sight
And now I can retrieve it not.
Since she who owns to it of right
Has none to give, and where's it sought?
How little it seems to those who see –
What would she want with me poor wretch? –
That without her nothing's here for me,
She lets me die who've no help left.

Since with my lady there's no use
In prayers, her pity, or pleading law,
Nor is she pleased at the news
I love her: then I'll say no more,
And so depart and swear it's done!
I'm dead: by death I'll answer her,
And off I'll go: she'll see me gone,
To wretched exile, who knows where?

Tristram, none will hear of me:
Off I'll go, who knows where?
I'll sing no more, resigned I'll be,
And banish joy and love of her.

Note: *Pound adapts and utilises phrases from verse 1,* 'qual cor mi vai: that goes to my heart' *at the start of Canto XCI;* 'es laissa cader: lets fall' *and* 'de joi sas alas: with joy, its wings' *in Notes for Canto CXVII et seq.*

TANT AI MO COR PLE DE JOYA

So full is my heart of joy now,
All is changed for me.
Flowering red, white, and yellow,
The winter seems to be,
For, with the wind and rain, so
My fortune's bright I see,
My songs they rise, and grow
My worth proportionately.
Such love in my heart I find,
Such joy and sweetness mine,
Ice turns to flowers fine
And snow to greenery.

I go without my clothes now,
One thin shirt for me,
For noble love protects now
From the chilly breeze.
But he's mad who'll not follow
Custom and harmony,
So I've taken care I vow
Since I sought to be
Lover of loveliest,
To be with honour blest:
Of her riches I'd not divest
For Pisa, for Italy.

From her friendship I'm severed
Yet my faith's so in place,
That I can barely counter
The beauty of her face.
I cannot hope to wed here
Such happiness and grace,
On the day when I see her
Weightlessness I taste.
To Love my heart's as near
As body to spirit clear,
Though she is far from here,
Fair France where I am placed.

I'm full of hope that's true now.
But that's little use to me,
She holds me in suspense I vow
Like a ship upon the sea.
From sad thoughts that follow,
I cannot win free.
Each night, head on pillow,
I turn fretfully.
More pain of love I suffer
Than Tristan the lover,
Who felt much dolour
For Iseult, her beauty.

Oh God were I a swallow
Flying through the air,
Rising from the depths below
Where I now despair.
Sweet and joyous lady, know
Without your loving, there,
I die, my heart it breaks so
The pulse is scarcely there.
My lady for your grace
I clasp my hands and pray
Lithe body and fresh face,
Have brought me many a care.

The world and its affairs
Could not absorb me so,
That when men spoke of her
My heart it would not glow,
My face not brighten there.
When I speak of her also
You'll quickly judge I care
Seeing my laughter grow.
My love for her's so deep
Often too I must weep,
So that my sighs taste sweet
Sweeter for tears they share.

Messenger, go now, fleet
Of foot, tell those you meet
Of all the pain and grief
It brings, the suffering I bear.

CAN PAR LA FLORS JOSTA.L VERT FOLH

When flowers are in the leaves green
And the sky's serene and clear,
And the song of birds rings keen,
Sweetening my heart, as I wake here,
Then since birds sing with their art
I who have greater joy at heart,
Must sing true, since my daily bread
Is joy and song, all that's in my head.

She whom I want most on this earth,
And love the more with heart and faith,
She joys to hear and keep my words,
Gathers and stores my pleas always.
And if men die by true love's art,
Then I must die, since in my heart
I bear her love, so true and fine,
All are false to one whom she'll loyal find.

I know when I retire at night
That I shall barely sleep a wink.
My sleep I lose, forego it quite
For you, my lady, as I think!
And where a man hides his treasure
There will his heart reside forever.
Lady I can't leave, if I see you not,
No sight is worth the beauty of my thought.

When I recall how I loved so
One who was false, without mercy,
I tell you such sorrow I did know
There was no path to joy for me.
Lady, for whom I sing and more,
Your lips wounded me to the core,
With a sweet kiss of love heart-true,
Grant joy, save me from mortal sorrow too.

Such as the proudest hearts may feel
When great joy or great good they see!
But I a finer spirit reveal,
And truer when God is good to me.
For when I'm on the fringes of love,
From fringe to centre then I move.
Thanks, lady: no one equals me.
I lack not, if God saves you for me.

Lady, if I should see you not,
Do not grieve more than I grieve,
Know well I see you in my heart!
He strikes at you because of me.
But if he strikes through jealousy,
Take care the heart he cannot reach.
If he vex you, annoy him too,
Then he'll not win good for ill from you.

God, guard my Sweet-Sight from harm
Whether I'm near to her or far.
God, my lady and Sweet-Sight save,
That's all I wish, no more I crave.

Note: *Pound adapts the last lines of verse 3* S'eu no vos vei, domna, don plus me cal, Negus vezers mo bel pesar no val' *as* 'And if I see *her* not…no sight is worth the beauty of my thought' *in Canto XX.*

CAN LA FREJ'AURA VENTA

When fresh breezes gather,
That from your country rise,
I seem to feel no other
Air but that of Paradise,
Through love of a lover
Who binds me with love's ties,
Where my will I tether,
And my true heart lies,
All others I despise,
But her who draws me ever!

If of her beauty present
Her clear face and sweet eyes,
I'd seen that merest content,
I'd still feel this surprise.
Deceit's not my intent,
For I've naught to realise;
Yet why should I repent,
For once she said, with sighs,
'On the true man love relies,
While the weak twig is bent'.

Women it seems to me
Make a great mistake,
By which true love is rarely
Returned for true love's sake.
I ought to speak out freely
With words though that will take,
For it can scarcely please me
When the tricksters rake
More love in than is at stake
For the lover who loves truly.

Lady what will you do
With me who loves you so?
Would you treat me so ill I too
Die of longing? Oh,
Good and noble, you,
Your face should sweeter show,
Light my heart through and through!
Great pain I suffer and woe,
Yet merit no hurt, ah no,
For I can't turn from you.

If there were none to annoy,
No vile slanderer, or thief,
Then love I might employ
But they cast it in my teeth:
It's human to care and not be coy,
On occasion, and seek relief,
But it's privately my belief
Pain has no other alloy
Than 'Good luck lives in joy,
And bad luck lives in grief.'

I am not one to disdain
The good that God may do,
For in that week, the very same
That I came away, it's true,
She said clearly, saying my name,
That my songs please her too.
Would all Christians plain
Could have such joy anew,
As I felt, and feel all through,
For all else but this is vain.

I'll believe her again
If she assures me it's true;
But if it's not, I'll disdain
To trust her, and you, and you.

'Fortune with her wheel'
Valerius Maximus,
translated by Simon de Hesdin and Nicolas de Gonesse
Les Fais et les Dis des Romains et de Autres Gens, vol. 1,
c. 1460 - 1487

CAN LA VERZ FOLHA S'ESPAN

When the greenery unfolds
And the branch is white with flower,
With sweet birdsong in that hour
My heart gently onward goes.
When I see the blossoming trees
And hear the nightingale in song,
Then how can a man go wrong,
Who chooses loving and is pleased.
For I have one I've chosen
Who gives me strength and joy.

And if all the world now holds –
All those under heaven's power,
Were gathered in some sweet bower,
I'd only wish for one I know.
Only she my heart can please,
Who makes me sigh all day long,
So at night my sleep is gone,
Not that I desire to sleep.
She, the slender dainty one,
True heart, does true speech employ.

If I were brought to her stronghold,
Prisoned by her in some tower,
And daily ate my morsel sour,
Happily I'd there grow old,
If my desire she granted me!
She should try to do no wrong:
If she made me yearn too long,
Neither life nor death I'd see:
Life for me as good as done,
While there with death I'd sadly toy.

PEL DOUTZ CHAN QUE·L ROSSINHOLS FAI

To the sweet song of the nightingale,
At night when I am half-asleep,
I wake possessed by joy complete,
Contemplating love and thinking;
For this is my greatest need, to be
Forever filled with joy and sweetly,
And in joy begin my singing.

Who seeks to know the joy I feel,
If such joy were heard and seen,
All other joy but slight would seem
Compared with mine: vast in its being.
Others preen and chatter wildly,
Claim to be blessed, rich and nobly,
With 'true love': I've twice the thing!

When I admire her body hale
Well-formed, in all respects I mean,
Her courtesy and her sweet speech,
For all my praise I yet gain nothing;
Though I took a year completely
I could not paint her truthfully
So courtly is she, of sweet forming.

You who think that I can't fail,
Not realising her spirit keen
Is open and is friendly, even
Yet her body is far from being,
Know, the best messenger I see
From her is my own reverie,
That recalls her fairest seeming.

Lady, I'm yours, today, every day,
In your service my self I'll keep,
Sworn, and pledged to you complete,
As I have been always in everything.
And as you are first of joys to me,
So the last joy too you will be,
As long as I'm still living.

I know not when I'll see you again;
But I am grieved and sad to leave.
For you I spurned (don't now harm me,
I beg of you) the court and king,
Now I will serve you there entirely,
Among the knights, among the ladies,
All sweet, true, and humble beings.

Huguet, my messenger, go, kindly
Sing my song and sing it freely,
To the Norman Queen go warbling.

Note: '*True love*' *in verse two, is* fins amor, *noble love, the troubadour ideal.*

'Knights'
Livy, translated by Pierre Bersuire, Ab urbe condita (Les
decades de Titus Livius), last decade of the 14th century

LA ROSSINHOLS S'ESBAUDEYA

The nightingale sings happily
Hard by the blossom on the bough,
And I am taken by such envy
I can't help but sing any how;
Knowing not what or whom either,
For I love not I, nor another.
Such effort I make that this will prove
Good verse too, though I'm not in love!

They gain more from love who pay
Court by deceiving, in their pride,
Than he who humbly makes his way,
And ever the suppliant does abide,
For Amor has no love for the man
Who is honest and noble as I am.
My loss is all the more complete,
That I am not false nor use deceit.

But as the bough bends beneath
The tempest that makes it sway,
I did to her my whole will bequeath,
She who assails me every way.
So she maddens and destroys me,
Sunk to low-born acts, completely,
Yet I'll give her my eyes to blind,
If any wrong she in me can find.

She often accuses me and tries me,
And lays false charges now, at will,
Yet whenever she acts vilely
All the fault's laid at my door still!
She quietly makes sport of me,
With her own faults damning me!
Truly they say, and it's my belief:
'All are my brothers!' cries the thief.

No man who sees her and has faith
In her sweet looks, her lovely eyes;
Could ever believe, in any way
Her heart is evil: her mind, it lies:
But waters that slide calmly by
Drown more than those that roar and sigh.
They deceive who seem so fair,
Oh, be wary of the debonair.

From every place she might be
I absent myself most carefully,
And so as not her form to see
I pass, eyes closed, and nervously.
So he follows Love, who avoids it,
And it pursues the man who flees it.
But I'm determined to pass it by,
Till I see it again in my lady's eye.

That will not be, if she torments me,
Peace and a truce are all I'm asking,
For it grieves me to exit limply,
And lose the good of all this suffering.
May she guard me and keep me hers,
And if we are not mutual lovers,
No other love it seems will shine
As bright to light this heart of mine.

As I am, would he were taken too,
My Auvergnat, then we'd make two,
For he could no more fare
Far from Bel Vezer of Beaucaire.

Tristan, though it seem not so to you,
Yet I love you more than I used to do.

CAN L'ERBA FRESCH'E·LH FOLHA PAR

When fresh leaves and shoots appear,
And the blossom gleams on the bough,
And the nightingale high and clear
Raises his voice, and sings aloud,
I joy in him, and enjoy the flowers,
And joy in my lady and I, for hours;
By joy on all sides I'm caught and bound,
But this is joy, and all other joys drowned.

Alas, how I die of musing deeply!
Many a time I'm so deep in thought,
Ruffians could abduct me, neatly,
And of the business I'd know naught.
By God, Love, you find me an easy matter,
With few friends, and no other master.
Why did you not constrain my lady
Before desire took me completely?

I marvel now how I can bear
Not to reveal to her my longing.
For when I behold my lady there,
Her lovely eyes are so charming
I can scarce stop myself running to her.
And so I would, were it not for fear,
For never has one so shaped and made
For love such diffidence displayed.

I love my lady and hold her dear,
And dread her, and respect her so,
I never dare speak of myself for fear,
Nor seek anything, nor ask aught, no;
Yet she knows of my pain and dolour,
And, when it pleases her, does me honour,
And, when it pleases her, I do with less,
So no reproach worsens my distress.

If I could work the enchanter's spell,
I'd make children of all my foes,
So none could ever spy or tell,
Nor do aught that might harm us both.
Then I'd know I'd see my noble one,
Her sweet eyes, fresh complexion,
And kiss her mouth in such a way
It would show for a month and a day.

It would be sweet to find her alone,
While she slept, or pretended to,
Then a sweet kiss I'd make my own,
Since I'm not worthy to ask for two.
By God, lady, little of love we've won!
Time goes by, and the best is done.
We need secret signs, you and I:
Boldness fails, so let cunning try!

A man should blame his lady indeed,
When she deters him from loving,
For endless talk about love may breed
Boredom, and set deception weaving.
For one can love and lie elsewhere,
And lie all the more smoothly where
There's no proof. Good lady deign
To love me, and I'll not lie or feign.

Go, messenger, no less esteem me
If I'm afraid to go see my lady.

LO TEMS VAI E VEN E VIRE

Time comes, and goes, and runs away,
In days, and months, and so in years;
And I, alas, have naught to say,
For my longing ever one appears.
It's ever one, and never falters,
For I love one, it never alters,
Of whom I've had no happiness.

Since she mocks me every way,
Grief and harm have come to me;
She has sat me down to play
At a game where I lose doubly –
For that love has always died
That's only upheld on one side –
Unless she make peace, I confess.

I should indeed lay the blame
On myself, with all due reason,
For never was born one so lame,
Who serves idly, in every season.
And if she'll not chase folly away
My folly will double, for they say:
A fool fears not till he's in distress.

I will be a singer no more,
Nor be of Lord Eble's school,
For what is all this singing for?
There's no worth in melody's rule;
Whatever I do, whatever I say
I can't make things go my way,
Nor do I dream of any progress.

Though I make a show of joy,
My heart within is full of woe.
Who ever did penance employ
Before he sinned? I tell you though,
The more I beg, the harsher she,
If she's not gentler soon with me,
There'll be a parting I would guess.

Yet it's good that she subjects me
To her whole will utterly,
For if she does wrong, and slowly,
The sooner she'll take pity;
For, or so the scriptures say,
Through good luck, a single day
May a whole century redress.

Lifelong, I'll never leave her,
As long as I'm hale and whole;
The flesh may go hang after
It has parted from the soul;
And though she is never hasty,
She'll get no blame from me,
If she makes amends, I'll bless.

Ah, sweet love, all my desire,
Fine, slim, neat your body stands,
Fresh complexion, subtle fire,
Whom God shaped in his hands!
I'll long for you forever,
No other gives me pleasure.
No other love do I profess.

Sweet and most gracious treasure,
May He who formed you in measure
Grant joy desired, now, in excess!

LA DOUZA VOTZ AI AUZIDA

The sweetest voice I have heard,
Of the woodland nightingale,
And into my heart has leapt its word
So that all the weight of care
And the evil blows love deals me,
Are soothed and softened sweetly.
And great good does it do me there,
Another's joy in my travail.

Of base life indeed is the man
Who with joy finds never a place,
Where love is no part of the plan
That drives his heart and his desire;
For all that exists with joy abounds,
Rings out, and with its song resounds:
Park, orchard, meadow, all the choir
Of heath, plain and woodland chase.

Alas for me, whom love forgets,
Who stray from the proper track;
A share of joy would be mine yet,
But sorrow it is that troubles me;
And I can find no place to rest,
For it turns all joy to bitterness.
And never think that I feel lightly,
If some courtesy I seem to lack.

A false and a wicked woman,
Of base birth, a foul traitress,
Betrayed herself and this man,
She cut the very stick that beat her.
Yet whenever she is arraigned
It is the man who gets the blame.
And the latecomer gets more from her,
Than I who have waited longest.

I had served her well and nobly,
Till she showed me a fickle heart;
And since she offers naught to me,
I'm a fool if I serve her more.
Service without recompense –
A Breton's hope has equal sense –
Makes a slave of a noble lord,
By custom and usage, set apart.

God grant him a foul fate
Who repeats men's idle chatter!
For love's joy were my estate
Were it not for the tellers of tales.
A fool treats his mistress cruelly,
I'll pardon her if she'll pardon me,
Liars they are, whom naught avails,
If they made me speak badly of her.

Corona, carry these verses for me
To Narbonne, there, to my lady;
Of perfection her life never fails,
And no man can speak badly of her.

CHANTARS NO POT GAIRE VALER

Singing proves merely valueless
If the song moves not from the heart,
Nor from the heart can song progress,
If it lacks noble love, heart's dream.
So of all songs mine reign supreme,
For with love's joy I seek to bind
Mouth, and eyes, and heart, and mind.

May God never grant me power
Not inspired by true love's art!
If I never knew how to gain its flower,
Without every day enduring pain,
I'd be of good heart still, that's plain,
And my joy is therefore more alive,
Since I'm of good heart, and for it I strive.

Through ignorance, the fools decry
Love, but that does it little hurt,
For Love will in no way fail, say I,
If it's a love that's not commonplace.
And that's not love, nor of its race,
But only has its form and name,
That loves nothing except for gain.

If I am to speak only what's true,
I know from where such errors start:
From those women who love men too
Only through greed: they are for hire.
Would I were false in this, a liar!
I speak of it, do I not, so harshly,
And yet that I lie not saddens me.

In its agreement and its assent
Two noble lovers love's apart,
For nothing can come of their intent,
If their desire is not mutual.
And he is in truth a natural
Who reprehends her for her longing,
Or praises to her what is not fitting.

My good hope is rightly placed,
When she from whom I'd least wish to part,
Shows me her beauteous face,
Pure, gentle, noble and true,
A king's salvation she'd prove too,
Lovely, graceful, of pleasing body;
I, with nothing, she renders wealthy.

I love and fear naught more than her,
I would receive the bitterest dart,
If only it gave my lady pleasure;
For it seems like Christmas Day
If her sweet spiritual eyes should stray
Towards me: yet so infrequently,
That each day's like a hundred to me!

Fine, natural verse, and good, I say,
To him who can clearly understand it,
If he hopes for joy, the better the fit.

Bernard de Ventadour understands it,
Speaks it; makes it, and wishes joy of it.

PEIRE D'AUVERGNE (FL.1157 - 1170)

 townsman's son from the Bishopric of Clermont-Ferrand, Peire d'Alvernhe was a professional troubadour. He was at the court of Sancho III of Castile in 1157-58, and appears at Piuvert in the Aude in 1170.

AB FINA JOIA COMENSSA

With noble joy commences
This verse that rhymes sweet words,
Where nothing harms the senses;
Yet I'd rather none might learn them
If my song does not concern them:
For may no wretched singer there,
Who'd render any song absurd,
Turn my sweet tune to braying.

Of Love I have remembrance
And its sweet speech: no more;
But by patient attendance
I hope joy will come my way.
Life demands as much, I say,
Since often, with a little care,
Things are better than before,
And we eat well without paying.

I've fine semblance of her favour
For with grace she welcomes me,
But otherwise not a savour,
Nor indeed should I aim so high,
Nor such rich joy accrue that I
Then feel like an emperor.
It's enough that she speaks to me,
And listens to what I'm saying.

In me she inspires such reticence,
For of herself so little she gives;
Joy which displays such diffidence,
Hardly puts a man at his ease.
Yet let her retain me, as she please,
For my suffering is not so rare.
I'll not reproach her, as she lives,
My love there's no dismaying.

I've done penance without sinning,
And it's wrong if I'm not forgiven;
For I set my heart, from the beginning,
On her mercy, though she grant it not.
I think ill will take me, for hope forgot
May lead a poor lover to despair.
As I have hope of being shriven,
In our Lord's name, hear me praying.

Assured of every worthiness,
Is my person, if she ennobles me,
Through whom is merit in excess,
And he's a fool who would suggest,
That any other should grant me rest.
No sweeter a daughter anywhere,
By as much as the weather's stormy,
Through Adam's lineage went straying.

I commend to the Counts of Provençe
This verse, and here at Narbonne,
Where joy has its cognisance,
My thanks to those by whom it reigns.
For here I find one who retains
Me as her lover, my lady fair;
Not in the fashion of some Gascon,
But in our own way we're playing.

RAIMBAUT D'ORANGE (C. 1144 - D. 1173)

aimbaut, Lord of Orange, Corethezon and other lands in Provençe and Languedoc, was the first troubadour originating from Provençe proper. As a minor, he was a ward of the lords of Baux and Marseilles. He died in 1173, possibly a victim of the widespread epidemic of that year.

AR RESPLAN LA FLORS ENVERSA

Now the flowers gleam, in reverse,

Among the jagged peaks and hills.

What flowers? Of snow, frost, and ice,

That jagged cut, and wound, and sting;

And dead the calls, cries, trills and whistles,

Among the twigs, and leafless bristles.

Yet joy is green: with joyous face,

I see the low shrivelled, and the base.

For in such a way do I reverse
All this, that fine plains look like hills,
I take for flowers the frost and ice,
In the cold I'm warm as anything,
And thunderclaps are songs and whistles,
And full of leaf the leafless bristles.
With joy I'm firmly bound in place,
Seeing nothing that's low or base,

Except a people, born our reverse,
As though nourished on the hills,
Who serve me worse than frost and ice,
For each one with his tongue can sting,
And murmurs evilly and whistles.
Sticks are no good or sharpened bristles,
Or threats; it's a joy to them, that race,
When they can do what men call base.

From kissing you, though I meet reverse,
No plains prevent me nor do hills,
Lady, nor do the frost and ice,
But powerlessness, ah, that's the thing.
Lady, for whom I sing and whistle,
Your lovely gaze, like sharpened bristle,
So chastens me with joy, no trace
Dare I own of low desire or base.

I have forged onwards in reverse,
Searching peaks, ravines and hills,
Like one tortured by frost and ice,
Whom the cold torments and stings,
So that no more would song or whistle
Rule me than lawless monks the bristle.
But now, Praise God, joy holds, a space,
Despite the slanderers, false and base.

May my verse, which I so reverse
That it's unhindered by woods or hills,
Go, where one feels not frost or ice,
Nor does the cold have power to sting.
To my mistress may he sing and whistle,
Clear, so her heart feels the sharp bristle,
Who can sing nobly, with joy and grace,
For it suits no singer vile and base.

Sweet lady, may love, joy, and grace
Unite us two, despite the base.

Jongleur, less joy is in this place,
For, unseen, I fear lest you are base.

NON CHANT PER AUZEL NI PER FLOR

I do not sing for bird or flower,
Nor for snow, now, nor for ice,
Nor for warmth or the cold's power,
Nor for the fields' fresh paradise;
Nor for any pleasure do I sing
Nor indeed have I been a singer,
But for my mistress, all my longing,
For on earth none lovelier may linger.

Now have I parted from one worse
Than any ever seen or found,
To love the fairest one on earth,
The lady of most worth, I'm bound.
And this I'll do my whole life long,
For I'm in love with no other;
And I believe her liking's strong
For me, so it seems to me her lover.

Lady, I shall have much honour
If ever the privilege is granted
Of clasping you beneath the cover,
Holding you naked as I've wanted;
For you are worth the hundred best,
And I'm not exaggerating either.
In that alone is my joy expressed,
More than if I were the emperor!

I'll make my mistress my lord and lady,
Whatever may be the outcome now,
For I drank that secret love, fatally,
And must love you evermore, I vow.
Tristan, when Iseult the Fair, his lover,
Granted his love, he could do no less,
And by such covenant I so love her,
I cannot escape it: she's my mistress.

I'd earn more worth than any other,
If such a nightgown were given me
As Iseult handed to her lover,
For it was never worn, certainly.
Tristan, you prized that noble gift:
And I am seeking for such another.
If she I long for grants me her shift,
I'll cease to envy you, fair brother!

See, lady, how God gives his aid
To she who of love is not afraid:
For Iseult stood there in great dread,
Then in a moment her heart said:
Convince your husband to believe
That no man born of woman may,
Claim he has touched you: I grieve
You can say the same of me today!

Carestia, don't you dare to leave
That place without bringing away
Part of the joy that she can weave
Who grants me more joy than I can say.

BEATRITZ DE DIA (C. 1140 - FL. C. 1175)

nown only as the *Comtessa de Dia*, the Countess of Diá, in contemporary documents, she was almost certainly named Beatriz, and probably the daughter of Count Isoard II of Diá north-east of Montelimar. According to her *vida*, she was married to Guillem or Guilhem de Poitiers, Count of Viennois, but was in love with and sang about Raimbaut of Orange, 1146-1173. Her song *A chantar m'er de so qu'eu no volria* is the only *canso* by a *trobairitz*, or female troubadour, to survive with its music intact. The score is found in *Le manuscript di roi*, a collection of songs copied circa 1270 for Charles of Anjou, the brother of Louis IX.

ESTAT AI EN GREU COSSIRIER

I've been in great distress of mind,

About a knight whom I possessed,

How I've loved him to excess

I want known, throughout all time;

Now I feel myself betrayed

Because I did not tell my love,

In great torment so I prove,

In bed or in my clothes arrayed.

Would that I might hold my knight
Till morning naked in my arms,
Intoxicated by my charms
He'd think himself in paradise;
For more pleased with him am I
Than Floris was with Blancheflor:
I grant him my heart, my amour,
My eyes, my mind, and my life.

Sweet friend, so good so gracious
When shall I have you in my power,
And lie with you at midnight hour,
And grant you kisses amorous?
Know, great desire I nurture too
To have you in my husband's place,
As soon as you grant me, with grace,
To do all that I'd have you do.

Note: *Floris and Blancheflor are* **Floris and Blancheflour** *lovers in a popular romance found in many different vernacular languages and versions. It first appears in Europe around 1160 in 'aristocratic' French, and was popular well into the fourteenth century. The poem tells of the troubles of two lovers: Blancheflour, or Blancheflor ('white flower') being a Christian princess abducted by Saracens and raised with the pagan prince Flores or Floris or Floire ('belonging to the flower') The Muslim/Christian tale is often set in Andalusia where there is a famous Granadan variant.* Aucassin and Nicolette *has a similar context.*

A CHANTAR M'ER DE SO QU'IEU NO VOLRIA

Now I must sing of what I would not do,
Complain of him I confess to loving true;
I love him more than any the world can view:
Yet my grace and courtesy own no value,
Nor my beauty, my worthiness, my mind;
I'm deceived, betrayed, as would be my due,
If the slightest charm in me he failed to find.

I solace myself with this, I was false never
My friend, to you, neither in acts nor manner;
I love you more than Seguis loved Valensa;
To conquer you in love gives me more pleasure,
Dear friend, for, of all, you are the worthiest;
Yet proud to me in deeds and what you utter,
Though you seem humble towards all the rest.

I marvel at the pride your heart dares display
To me, friend, the cause why I weep all day,
And it's wrong that another draws you away,
Whatever she does, whatever she might say,
And however it may recall the true beginning
Of our love: the good God wishes in no way
That any fault of mine should cause its ending.

From the great gallantry lodged in your heart,
And the rich worth you own, my torments start;
For I know no lady near to you or afar,
Desiring love, who towards you would not draw:
Yet you, dear friend, are of such fine judgement
You ought to know who the sincerest are;
And remember, remember our agreement.

My worth should help me and my nobility,
My beauty, and more my own heart's loyalty;
That's why I send now, wherever you may be,
This song to act as a messenger from me;
I wish to know, my sweet and gentle friend,
Why to me so harsh and full of cruelty;
I'd know if it's pride, or ill-will in the end.

And I'd have him say, this messenger I send,
That excess of pride works harm on many men.

Notes: *Seguis and Valenca, or Seguin and Valence, a pair of lovers in a lost romance, are mentioned also by Arnaut de Mareuil.*

The covinens, *the 'agreement', mentioned at the end of the fourth verse is the standard term for the concordia that ended conflicts in eleventh and twelfth-century Occitania. Here it is used to reinforce the sense of a binding love.*

ARNAUT DE MAREUIL (LATE 12TH CENTURY)

he name is spelt variously, from Maroil, to Miroilh. The vida has Arnaut as a poor clerk from the castle of Mareuil in Perigord. He was a joglar at the court of the Countess of Burlatz, Azalais of Toulouse, daughter of Count Raimon V. In 1171 she married Roger II, Viscount of Beziers and Cacassonne, called Talliafero, or Taillefer. She was loved by Alfons II of Aragon, d.1196. Arnaut was dismissed, and found refuge with Guillem VIII de Montpellier, d.1202, a noted sponsor of joglars.

BEL M'ES QUAN LO VENS M'ALENA

It's sweet when the breeze blows softly,
As April turns into May,
And in tranquil night above me,
Sing the nightingale and jay.

When each bird in his sweet language,
In the freshness of the morn
Sings, joyful of his advantage,
At ease with his mate, at dawn.

As all things on earth have joy so,
Are happy when leaves appear,
Then I'll recall a love I know
And rejoice in all the year.

By past usage and by nature,
It seems now that I must turn
Where soft winds revive the creature,
And heart must dream and yearn.

Whiter she is than Helen was,
The loveliest flower of May,
Full of courtesy, sweet lips she has,
And ever true word does say.

Open-hearted, her manner free,
Fresh colour and golden hair,
God who grants her all sovereignty
Preserve her, the best is there.

I'd be blessed, if she'd not treat me
To endless quarrelling here,
But grant me a kiss discretely
For my service costs me dear.

Then we'd go on a brief journey,
Often, a fine short play;
For her sweet body has led me
Willingly on that way.

ARNAUT DANIEL (FL. 1180 - 1210)

rnaut Danièl de Riberac, of Ribeyrac in Périgord, was praised, in Dante's Purgatorio, by Guido Guinicelli, as *il miglior fabbro*, the better maker, and called the Grand Master of Love by Petrarch. Riberac is on the left bank of the Dronne in the Dordogne.

'Ieu sui Arnautz qu'amas l'aura
e chatz la lebre ab lo bueu
e nadi contra suberna.'

'I am Arnaut who nets the breeze
and with an ox pursues the hare
and swims against the rising seas.'

SOLS SUI QUI SAI LO SOBRAFAN QUE·M SORTZ

I am the one that knows the pain that flows
Through loving hearts that suffer love's excess,
For my desire is ever so firm and whole
I have never denied her, never wandered
From one I so desired at once and ever:
Far from her, now, I call to her urgently,
Though when she's here I know not what to say.

My blindness, my deafness to others shows
That only her I see, and hear, and bless,
And I offer her no false flatteries so,
For the heart more than the mouth gives word;
That in field, plain, hill, vale, though I go everywhere
I'd not discern all qualities in one sole body,
Only hers, where God sets them all today.

Many a goodly court my presence knows,
Yet in her there's more that does impress,
Measure and wit and other virtue glows
Beauty, youth, good manners, actions stir,
Of courtesy she has well-learnt her share
Of all displeasing things I find her free
I think no good thing lacking anyway.

No joy for me were too brief that arose
From her: I hope that she might guess,
For of me she'll otherwise not know,
Since the heart such words can scarce utter,
That the Rhone, its swollen waters there,
No fiercer than my heart flows inwardly,
Nor floods more with love, when on her I gaze.

Solace and joy seem false from those
Other girls, none share her worthiness,
Her solace exceeds all others though,
Ay, alas, ill times if I do not have her,
Yet the anguish brings me joy so fair,
For thinking brings desire of her lustily:
God, if I might have her some other way!

No play ever pleased more, you may suppose,

Nothing could bring the heart more happiness,

Than this, of which no evil rumours grow

All publicly, to me alone its treasure;

I speak too openly? Not if it brings no care:

My beauty, by God, I'd lose my tongue and speech,

Rather than trouble you by what I say.

And I pray my song indeed brings you no care,

For if you like both words and melody

What cares Arnaut whom it pleases or shall dismay.

QUAN CHAI LA FUEILHA

When the pale leaves descend
From the high crowns of trees
And the cold airs ascend,
Hazel and willow freeze,
To sweet melodies
The forest is then no friend,
Yet, who may flee,
I long for true Love again.

Though cold it grows,
I will not freeze forever,
In whom love rose
That will my heart deliver
I'll not shiver,
Love hides me from head to toe,
Brings strength rather
And tells me which way to go.

Good is this life
That my delight sustains
Though he who knows strife
May otherwise complain
I know no gain
In changing of my life
All free of pain,
By my faith's, my share of strife.

In true love-making
I find none here to blame,
With others, playing,
There's bad luck in the game,
There's none the same
As her, there's no repeating,
She's one I name
Beyond all equalling.

I'd not go giving
My heart to another love
Lest I find it fleeing
Or from her gaze remove;
I fear not too
That Malspina's rhyming,
Can prove
A nobler than her in seeming.

There's nothing bad there
In she who is my friend;
This side Savoy here
None finer I contend;
Joys without end
She gives and greater
Than Paris gained
In Troy from his Helena.

She is more lovely
She who brings delight,
Than the noble thirty
Finer in every light,
So it is right
That she hear my melody
For she's the height
Of worth, wins all praise truly.

My song take flight,
present yourself to her sweetly,
but for her might
Arnaut might strive more lightly.

'The conquest of Troy'
Histoire Universelle, second half of the 14th century

DOUZ BRAITZ E CRITZ

Sweet tweet and cry
Song, tune and trill,
Birds, in their language, hear tell their tale
Each to its mate, in just the way that we
Pray to the dear friends we love here:
So I that love the worthiest
Must make a song so far above the rest
It has no false rhyme, no word in error.

I did not stray, I
Felt no lack of will,
When I first entered the castle's pale,
Where is she I hunger for, my lady,
St Guillelm's nephew's ache was no greater:
A thousand times a day I yawn and stretch
Because of the lovely one, as much the best
As above that ague rates deepest pleasure.

I was well liked, no lie,
My words they left no chill,
No wise man but my choice must hail,
Not copper but pure gold pleased me,
That day I saw my lady, kissed her,
And she her lovely blue cloak pressed
Round me, to set snake-tongues at rest,
And hide what bad mouths deliver.

No branch alive
That bud and blossom fill
That bird's beak trembles like a gale,
Is fresher, no Rouen would suit me,
Or Jerusalem, without my lover,
Hands clasped, I yield to her I confess,
Dover's King her love would honour no less,
Or those of Estela and Pamplona.

God on high,
By whom was forgiven all ill
Committed by Longis, blind as a nail,
May He will that my love and I entwine sweetly,
In the room where we pledged to be together,
Rich pledge from which great joy I expect,
Her sweet body, smiling, kissing, to address,
And gaze at her against the light of the lamp, there.

What, Mouth, do you sigh?
I think you'll have robbed me, would still,
Of such promises as would entail
Honour even for the Emperor of Greece,
Rouen's lord, or Tyre and Bethlehem's ruler:
Yet a fool am I, seeking what I repent, excess,
Since Love has no power to protect me, and less
Wise is the man who does his joy dissever.

The merciless try,

With sharp tongues, poison to distil,

I fear them not, though Galicia's lord, men say,

They forced to sin, whom we may blame it seems

For capturing, on a pilgrimage fair,

The count's son Raymond, and in intent

King Ferdinand wins little true merit yet

If he'll not free nor return him ever.

I would have seen it, but I wait here yet:

I was at the crowning of the good king of Estampa.

Note: *Pound quotes part of verse 5 last line* 'E quel remir contral lums de la lampa' *in Canto VII.*

'Coronation ceremonies'
Chroniques de France ou de St Denis (from 1270 to 1380)
Last quarter of the 14th century

ER VEI VERMEILHS, VERTZ, BLAUS, BLANCS, GRUOCS

'I am Arnaut, who weeping goes and sings: seeing, gone by, the folly in my mind, joyful, I hope for what the new day brings…. Then he hid himself in the refining fire.'

– *Dante:* Purgatorio XXVI:*142-144, 148*

I see scarlet; green, blue, white, yellow
Garden, close, hill, valley and field,
And songs of birds echo and ring
In sweet accord, at evening and dawn:
They urge my heart to depict in song
Such a flower that its fruit will be amour,
And joy the seed, and the scent a foil to sadness.

The fire of Love burns in my thoughts so
That desire, always sweet and deep,
And its pains a certain savour bring,
And gentler its flame the more the passion:
For Love requires his friends to belong
To truth, frankness, faith, mercy and more,
For, at his court, pride fails while flattery's harmless.

I'm not altered by time and place though
Or what fate, advice, good or bad, may yield;
And if I give you the lie in anything
Never let her look on me night or morn,
She's in my heart, day-long and night-long,
Whom I'd not wish to lack (for false is the call)
On those shores where Alexander once proved ruthless.

Often my boredom without her I show
And I wish to tell, not leave concealed,
Of her at least some part of this thing,
Since my heart never wavers or is torn:
Since of aught else I never think for long,
Since of what's good I know she's best of all,
Seen in my heart, in Puglia or Flanders' fastness.

I'd wish simply to be her cook and, lo,
Thus receive such wages in that field
I'd live more than twenty years a king,
She makes me so happy, never forlorn:
Such a fool am I: for what do I long?
For I want none of those riches, not all
That Meander and Tigris enclose with all their vastness.

Amongst others I feign the status quo,
While the day seems tedium congealed:
And it grieves me the God of Everything
Won't let me cut short the time I mourn,
Since lovers languish, waiting over-long:
Moon and Sun your course begins to pall!
It grieves me your light so seldom yields to blackness.

Now go to her, my song, to her I belong,

For Arnaut cannot show her treasures all,

Much greater wit he'd need to reveal her richness.

Note: *Pound utilises an issue of translation regarding the last line of verse 1,* E jois le grans, e l'olors d'enoi gandres *in Canto XX.*

'The garden of Eden'
Book of Hours, Use of Paris (the 'Bedford Hours')
c. 1410 - 1430

ANC IEU NON L'AIC, MAS ELHA M'A

I have him not, yet he has me
Forever in his power, Amor,
And makes me sad, bright: wise, a fool,
Like one who can no way retreat.
He's no defence who loves indeed,
He obeys Love's decree
For he serves and woos her, she,
So I'll await | like fate
My gracious fee
Should it come to me.

I say little of what's inside me,
I tremble lest I shake with fear;
Tongue may feign, but heart wills too
That which it dwells on sadly:
So I languish, but silently,
For as totally
As earth's bordered by sea
None I may state | of late
Compares equally
To that coveted she.

I know her worth so certainly

That I can no way turn elsewhere;

Which simply makes my poor heart brood,

When sun sets or rises swiftly:

I dare not say who inflames me;

My heart burns me

But my eyes are fed surely,

To contemplate | will sate,

That alone can ease me:

What keeps me alive, now see!

He's a fool who in loose speech

Claims his pains with joy compare,

For slanderers, whom God makes fools,

Never such fancy language seek:

One whispers while another shrieks,

Till Love retreats

That else would be complete;

I obfuscate | debate,

While they bully,

And still love loyally.

But health and joy now fill me
With pleasure that rises there;
Yet from my throat won't issue
For fear she may prove angry,
Since the flame of it yet I feel,
Of Love, that orders me
Never my heart to reveal,
Oft a mistake | fears make,
Loves are lost, not few,
Through poor security.

How many songs light and easy
I'd have made if she would succour
She who gives me joy and takes it,
Now I'm glad, now I'm unhappy,
Because to her will she binds me;
Yet it will make never a plea,
My heart, nor will seek to flee,
But freely I'll state | meets fate:
Should she forget me,
Then fled is mercy.

Tell Miels-de-Ben, if she rate
This fair melody,
Arnaut keeps memory.

Note: *Regarding Miels-de-Ben, Better-than-Good, Arnaut's vida says:* Et amet una auta dompna de Gascoigna, moiller d'En Guillem de Buonvila, mas non fo crezut qez anc la dompna li fezes plazer en dreich d'amor. *'And he loved a noble woman of Gascony, wife of Lord Guillem de Buonvila, but it was not believed that she ever pleased him with regard to the rights of love.' Possibly this poem was addressed to her.*

LO FERM VOLER QU'EL COR M'INTRA

The firm desire that in my heart enters
Can't be torn away by beak or nail
Of slanderer, who'll by cursing lose his soul,
And since I don't dare strike with branch or rod,
Secretly, at least, where I'll have no uncle,
I'll take my joy, in orchard or in chamber.

When I bring to mind that chamber
Where I know to my cost no man enters –
More hostile they are to me than brother, uncle –
No part of me but shivers, to my very nail,
More than a little child that sees the rod,
Such my fear of being hers too much in soul.

Would I were hers in body, and not in soul,
And she admitted me secretly to her chamber!
For it wounds my heart more than blow from rod,
That where she is her servant never enters.
I would be close to her like flesh to nail,
And not heed the warning of friend or uncle.

Never have I loved sister of my uncle
Longer or more deeply, by my soul,
For, as close as is the finger to the nail,
If she pleased, would I be to her chamber.
More can love bend, that in my heart enters,
Me to its will, than the strong some frail rod.

Since there flowered the Dry Rod,
Or from Adam sprang nephew and uncle;
Such true love as that which my heart enters
Has never, I think, existed in body or soul:
Wherever she is, abroad or in some chamber,
My heart can't part from her more than a nail.

So clings to her, is fixed as with a nail,
My heart, as the bark cleaves to the rod,
She is of joy my tower, palace, chamber;
And I love her more than brother, or uncle:
And twice the joy in Paradise for my soul,
If any man there through true loving enters.

Arnaut sends out his song of nail and uncle,
For her joy, who arms him with rod, his soul,
His Desire, that with worth her chamber enters.

Notes: *Arnaut here invents the* sestina, *with its fixed set of words ending the lines of each of the six-line stanzas, but in a different order each time; numbering the first stanza's lines 123456, then the words ending the following stanzas appear in the order 615243, then 364125, then 532614, then 451362, and 246531. These six rhymes then appear in the* tercet *as well.*

The manuscript reading of the last two lines has proved contentious, a grat de lieis que de sa vergua l'arma, son Dezirat, c'ab pretz en cambra intra *is assumed. The subject of the verb 'enters' is then ambiguous. For 'uncle' read guardian, or keeper, throughout.*

The music for this sestina survives in manuscript.

EN CEST SONNET COIND'E LERI

To this light tune, graceful and slender,
I set words, and shape and plane them,
So they'll be both true and sure,
With a little touch, and the file's care;
For Amor gilds and smoothes the flow
Of my song she alone inspires,
Who nurtures worth and is my guide.

Each day I grow better, purer,
For I serve and adore the noblest woman
In all the world – so I claim, and more.
I'm hers from my feet to my hair,
And even if the cold winds blow
Love reigns in my heart, and it acquires
Heat that the deepest winters hide.

A thousand masses I hear and offer,
Burn oil, wax candles in my hand,
So that success God might ensure,
For striving alone won't climb her stair.
When I gaze on her hair's golden glow
And her body's fresh delicate fires,
I love her more than all else beside.

I love her deeply and long for her,
Fear desire may lose her, if one can
Prove loving too well a fatal flaw!
For her heart floods mine everywhere,
It never subsides, that tidal flow;
Usury gains her the man she hires:
Worker, workshop, and all inside.

I'd not wish to be Rome's Emperor,
Nor Pope, nor Luserna's castellan,
If I can't return and haunt her door,
For whom my heart must crackle and flare;
And if she soothes not pain and sorrow
With a kiss, before the year expires,
She'll have damned herself, and I'll have died.

Despite all the torment that I suffer
To renounce true love is not my plan,
Though I'm exiled to a desert shore,
These words shall rhyme the whole affair:
More than ploughmen, lovers toil so;
In the tale, Monclis no more admires
Audierna, than I for my love have sighed.

'I net the breeze, I am Arnaut,
Who with an ox the swift hare tires,
And swims against the rising tide.'

Notes: *I have altered the position of the reference to Luserna in the poem for clarity. Its location is unknown but might have been Lucena, northwest of Castellon in Valencia.*

Moncli (Monclis, Monclin, Mondis) and his lady, Audierna, are presumed to be characters in a lost romance.

I offer here an alternative translation of the tercet *to fulfil Arnaut's rhyming scheme according to my choice of end-rhymes. The original is far more musical, as you can gather from the text at the start of this selection of his verse.*

PEIRE VIDAL (1175 – 1205)

eputedly the son of a furrier, he started his career as a troubadour in the court of Raimon V of Toulouse and was also associated with Raimon Barral the Viscount of Marseille, King Alfonso II of Aragon, Boniface of Montferrat, and Manfred I Lancia. He may have taken part in the Third Crusade. Legend has it that he fled the court of Barral after stealing a kiss from his wife Alazais de Rocamartina, that is Roquemartine near Aix, and that he dressed in wolf-skins to woo Loba, the 'she-wolf', Loba de Penautier of Carcassonne, and was savaged by her dogs, and that he subsequently married the daughter of the Byzantine Emperor in Cyprus.

AB L'ALEN TIR VAS ME L'AIRE

I breathe deeply, draw in the air,
That blows here from Provençe!
It pleases me, all I countenance
From there: if good report I hear,
I listen smiling to all that's said,
And for one word ask a hundred:
So good it is to hear good things.

There's no place so sweet as there
From the Rhone as far as Vence,
Between the sea and the Durance,
There's no such sweet joy anywhere.
So that with that true race I find,
I've left my joyful heart behind,
With her who leaves men smiling.

Let no man say the day's not fair
That leaves of her a memory,
Of her joy's born, by her set free.
And whatever man praises her,
Speaks well of her, he tells no lie!
For she's the best, all men say ay,
And the noblest of all existing.

And if I can speak and do my share,
I've her to thank, who every learning
Granted me, and all understanding,
And made me a singer debonair,
And anything I make that's fine,
From her sweet lovely body's mine,
True-hearted thought including.

GES QUAR ESTIUS

Though spring's glorious
Lovely and sweet,
I'm not complete,
Painful defeat
Is mine today,
Through her who holds my heart in play;
So I prize not April or May,
For she blithely turns away
One I honour and love always.
And if I've lost my songs so sweet
Those fair words and fine melodies,
I used to make when love was there,
Happiness is I know not where.

Not once have I thus
Broken accord,
Order ignored,
Unless I'm floored,
Too low to grace
Her lovely body's dwelling place;
So I fear slanderers have their say,
Who cause ladies and lovers dismay,
Lower us, and drive all joy away,
And each and every way harm me.
Yet, as I hide my love cleverly,
My worth shall seem more than it is;
Still, opportunity I miss.

No Greek among us
Has dealt such pain
Cruelty plain,
I would maintain,
As that I've seen:
In such misery and fear I've been,
My eyes scarcely move it seems
When I see her, fear so extreme,
Sweet, gracious words lacking I mean.
Since with pleasure I'm out of tune,
And nothing can I force her to,
For I know that I'll win nothing,
Except by praising, and by loving.

People and rivers
I've sung their praise
Five hundred ways,
All of my days,
To those who treat me
Worse than they could, though you'd agree
They'll hear nothing but good from me.
And if I wished them to fare badly,
Then I could, may God preserve me,
Show pride and scorn towards them too;
It's not in my power so to do,
For at a smile and a glance,
I forget sorry circumstance.

Yet now it's grievous,

Conversation;

Death's my portion,

Sense and reason

Flee in the night;

Not one song I write,

I've lost the power to rhyme aright.

And since I've neither heart nor might,

How should I sing or find delight?

For from her there's no response,

And when I seek an amorous song,

It flies off, there's none to hear me:

See then how you must persuade me!

Ashamed among us

One's always grave,

Yet mercies save,

And orders brave

From heart that's true,

Bring joy to lovers through and through.

And he who takes what love brings too,

Though little it grant of hope's fine brew,

Cannot fail to find pleasures new

And in fresh joy rich recompense:

So that I praise the honours sent,

The gifts, neck, hands that make me kiss,

My remedy for all amiss.

My Vierna, bitter it is,
The sight of you I often miss.

Lord Agout, though scant praise is this,
You'll gild my song, such as it is.

PLUS QUE.L PAUBRES QUAN JAI EL RIC OSTAL

No more than a beggar dare complain,
Lodging at some rich man's address,
Fearing its lord, of his wretchedness;
No more dare I, of my mortal pain.
Since she disdains me, I must suffer,
Whom I long for more than another.
No more do I dare to ask her mercy,
So great my fear that she'll grow angry.

As we gaze in awe at some great window,
Shining in beauty against the splendour,
Seeing her, my heart so sweet is rendered
I forget myself in her beauty's glow.
With the stick I cut, Love brings me pain,
For, one day, in his royal domain,
I stole a kiss for the heart to remember:
Oh, for the man who can't see his lover!

God forgive, yet she's but a criminal
My lovely lady, who grants no aid,
Knowing my love, my heart, are laid
At her feet, and her service is my all.
Why summon me, and greet me so gently,
Then deny me good from all that hurts me!
Does she believe she might banish me so?
Yet the pain's no less than I used to know.

For a true man must endure, it's natural,
Rights and wrongs, both sense and folly:
Though it's hard to achieve a victory
When he's banished from his own hall!
I'm in exile if I should leave my lover:
I'll not: for I love her more than ever.
If I renounced her love, she'd scorn me:
She ought not, for love it is adorns me.

I'm utterly in my lady's power,
If she does me ill I can do nothing,
Her pleasure, to me, is so sweet and thing,
I forget myself, my cares, the hour.
Never a day but love drowns my heart,
Since arrows of joy from her eyes dart.
And when my heart thinks of its great good,
I want none else in this world, nor should.

Do you know why my love is so sincere?
I've seen none so noble, of such beauty,
Or so fine, who grants me such bounty,
For so worthy a friend she does appear,
And if I'd her naked at last beside me,
I'd be more than the lord of Excideuil,
Who maintains his worth where others fail,
For none but Geoffrey could so prevail.

It goes ill with the four kings of Spain,

Since they fight rather than make peace,

Do that, and their worth could but increase:

Free, loyal, courteous, they speak plain,

Yet their fame might be even greater

If they aimed their war against another,

That fierce foe that denies our law,

Until Spain owns to one faith once more.

Bels Castiat, lord, I'm sad, you'll gather.

I see you not: she sees me no more,

Na Vierna, who is all my faith and law.

Now I'll give the ancient saying here:

Whoever starts well then lets things fall,

Had better not start such things at all.

Notes: *The Lord of Exiceuil is Richard Coeur-de-Lion. Geoffrey is his brother, Count of Brittany.*

Castiatz is possibly Raimond V, Count of Toulouse (1148-1194)

Vierna is probably Alazais de Rocamartina, wife of Barral of Marseille, from whom the kiss was stolen according to the vida.

The four kings of Spain are those of Aragon, Castille, Léon and Navarre.

ESTAT AI GRAN SAZO

I've felt, for so long, so
Bitter, and known such pain,
But now I feel joy again,
More than carp or swallow,
For my lady tells me
Now again she'll take me,
Once more, as her lover.
Ah! How sweet the hour
When she deigned to will
I might enjoy hope still.

May God pardon me though,
My joy I can't regain,
Lest swiftly once again,
To that prison I go,
Where her beauty holds me,
There is all courtesy
There it's joyous and sweet;
Which is why I'm replete
Without earthly treasure,
Should I bring her pleasure.

How great my pleasure too,
When I can see her face;
I cease to know the place,
Her love-filled eyes in view;
I'm tangled then, and won,
Conquered and so undone,
Can't turn my eyes away,
Nor ever from her stray,
And when I can see her
All is joy for me there.

Lady, by God above,
Since I am yours wholly,
Willingly and humbly,
Grant me of your love,
Your mercy, and pity,
Your prayers, and loyalty,
And do yourself honour:
For I'm burdened by fear,
That I might not aspire
To one whom I desire.

And my heart's rancorous
Towards one who is evil,
Who sends me to the devil,
She, with her Count Rufous,
She's a wolf all over,
Now a count's her lover
Her emperor's on his way,
Who sang her praise all day,
Through the whole world too:
But liars never speak true.

God save the Marquis,
His lovely sister, save,
Her loyal love and brave,
It conquers me anew,
Better still holds me too.

King's daughter, be it so,
A false love fled away
I've a better one today,
Who knows my worth, and who
Does and says things sweet and true.

Notes: *The 'wolf' is Loba de Penautier. The* vida *claims that Vidal called himself Lop because of her and carried the badge of the wolf. He was hunted with dogs in the mountains of Cabaret, and wore a wolfskin to give the scent to the dogs and masters. He was hunted down, beaten and carried half-dead to Loba and her husband who laughed at his folly.*

The Count, her lover, was probably Roger of Foix (1188-1223).

The illustrious marquis and his sister are Boniface 1 Marquis of Montferrat and his sister Azalais who married Manfred II, Marquis of Saluces in 1182.

RAIMBAUT DE VAQUEIRAS
(C. 1155 - FL. 1180 - D. C1207)

aimbaut de Vaqueiras, or Riambaut de Vaqueyras, came from Vacqueyras near Orange, Vaucluse. He spent most of his career as court poet and close friend of Boniface I of Montferrat. He joined the Fourth Crusade in 1203 and was present at the siege of Constantinople in 1204. He is presumed to have died in an ambush by Bulgarian forces.

ALTAS ONDAS QUE VENEZ SUZ LA MAR

Deep waves that roll, travelling the sea,
That high winds, here and there, set free,
What news of my love do you bring to me?
What passes there? Never his ship, I see.

And ah, God of Amour!
Now you bring joy, and now dolour.

Ah, sweet breeze, from there, true, you sigh,
Where my love joys, sleeps, and suspires.
A sip of his sweet breath for me, send by.
My lips are parted, so deep my desires.

And ah, God of Amour!
Now you bring joy, and now dolour.

False love he makes, slave of a far country,
Now laughter and jests turn to misery.
I'd not dreamed my friend would ask of me
That I grant him such love as he did seek.

And ah, God of Amour!
Now you bring joy, and now dolour.

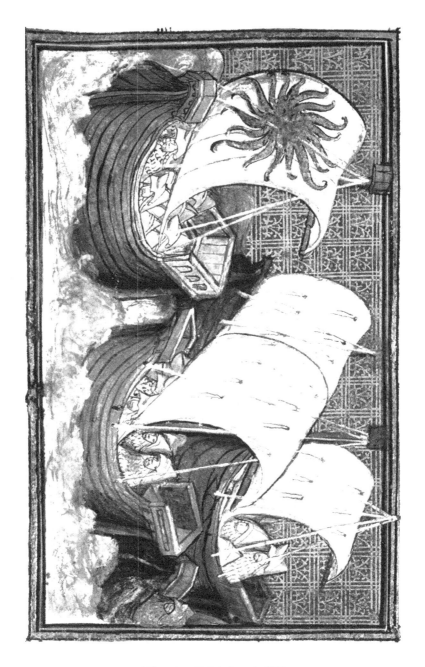

'Fleet of Richard II'
Jean Creton, La Prinse et Mort du Roy Richart
c. 1401 - c. 1405

GAITA BE, GAITETA DEL CHASTEL

Keep a watch, watchman there, on the wall,
While the best, loveliest of them all
    I have with me until the dawn.
    For the day comes without our call,
        New joys all,
        Lost to the dawn,
    The dawn, oh, the dawn!

Watch, friend, watch there, and call and cry,
I'm rich indeed, all I wish have I.
    But now I'm vexed by the dawn,
    And the sorrows, that day brings nigh,
        Make me sigh,
        More than the dawn
    The dawn, oh, the dawn!

Keep a watch, watchman there, on the tower,
For your lord: jealously he holds power,
    He's more vexing than the dawn:
    While words of love we speak here.
        But our fear
        Comes with the dawn,
    The dawn, oh, the dawn!

Lady, adieu! No longer dare I stay;
Despite my wish, I must be away.
> Yet heavily weighs the dawn,
> How soon we'll see the day;
>> To betray
>> Us, wills the dawn,
> The dawn, oh, the dawn!

KALENDA MAIA

Calends of May
Nor leafy spray
Nor songs of birds, nor flowers gay
Please me today
My Lady, nay,
Lest there's a fine message I pray
From your loveliness, to relay
The pleasures new love and joy may
Display
And I'll play
For you, true lady, I say,
And lay
By the way
The jealous ones, ere I go away.

My belle *amie*
Let it not be
That any man scorns me from jealousy,
He'd pay me,
Dearly indeed
If lovers were parted by such as he;
Never would I live happily,
No happiness without you I see;
I'd flee
Run free

No man would find me readily;

An end

Of me,

Fine Lady, were you lost utterly.

How could I lose her

Replace her ever

Any fine Lady, before I had her?

No beloved or lover

Is just a dreamer;

When he's a lover, no more a suitor,

He has accrued a signal honour,

A sweet glance produces such colours;

Yet I here

Have never

Held you naked, nor any other;

Longed for,

Lived for,

You without pay, I have though, forever.

I'd be sadder

Should we part ever,

Sorrowful, my Beautiful Warrior,

For my heart never

Seems to deliver

Me from desire

Nor slakes it further;

Gives pleasure only to the slanderer

He, my lady, who finds no other

Joy, the man there

Who'd feel my utter
Loss, and thanks would offer,
And consider
Insolent starer
You, the one from whom I suffer.

Flowers so kindly,
Over all brightly,
Noble Beatrice, and grows so sweetly
Your Honour to me;
For as I see,
Value adorns your sovereignty,
And, to be sure, the sweetest speech;
Of gracious deeds you are the seed;
Verity,
Mercy,
You have: and great learning truly;
Bravery
Plainly,
Decked, with your generosity.

Lady so graced,
All acclaimed and have praised
Your worth with pleasure freighted;
Who forgets, instead,
May as well be dead,
I adore, you, the ever-exalted;
Since you have the kindest head,
And are best, and the worthiest bred,
I've flattered

I've served

More truly than Érec Énida.

Words are fled,

All is said,

Sweet Engles – my *estampida*.

Notes: *The Calends, Latin* Kalendae, *corresponded to the first days of each month of the Roman calendar, signifying the start of the new moon cycle. The troubadours' spring celebrations of* kalenda maia *and their courtly worship of 'the lady' probably drew on remnants of pre-Christian worship. Pound mentions* Kalenda Maya *in Canto CXIII.*

Engles is Boniface Marquess of Montferrat (c1150-1207), leader of the Fourth Crusade, called here Engles, the 'Englishman', for some unknown reason. Beatrice was his eldest daughter.

Beatrice is probably Boniface's daughter Biatrix. The vida *claims that Raimbaut spied on Beatrice in her shift practising with her husband's sword, after which he called her his Bel Cavalier.*

Érec et Énide is Chrétien de Troyes' first romance, completed around 1170 and the earliest known Arthurian work in Old French. It tells the tale of Érec, one of Arthur's knights, and the conflict between love and knighthood he experiences in his marriage to Énide.

The Estampida, a medieval dance and musical form called the estampie *in French, and* istampitta *(also* istanpitta *or* stampita*) in Italian was a popular instrumental style of the 13th and 14th centuries. The earliest reported example of the musical form is this song* Kalenda Maya, *supposedly written to the melody of an estampida played by French jongleurs. All other known examples are purely instrumental pieces.*

GUILLEM DE CABESTAN (1162 – 1212)

 Catalan from Capestany in the County of Roussillon, his name in Occitan is Guilhem de Cabestaing, Cabestang, Cabestan, or Cabestanh. According to his legendary *vida*, he was the lover of Seremonda, or Soremonda, wife of Raimon of Castel Rossillon. Raimon killed Cabestan, and fed the lover's heart to her without her knowledge. On discovering what she had eaten, she threw herself from a window to her death. The legend appears later in Boccaccio's *Decameron*.

"It is Cabestan's heart in the dish!"

– Ezra Pound, Canto IV

AISSI CUM SELH QUE BAISSA·L FUELH

Like to him who bends the leaves
And picks the loveliest flower of all
I from the highest branch have seized,
Of them, the one most beautiful,
One God has made, without a stain,
Made her out of His own beauty,
And He commanded that humility
Should her great worth grace again.

With her sweet glance, her gentle eyes
She made true joyous lover of me,
And the love whose pain applies
Heart's tears to my complexion, see,
I have never sought to explain;
But now I'll sing of her freely,
From whom is born such beauty
For I've not shown her plain.

I won't speak common boasts or praise,
But truth, with a thousand witnesses,
Let all desire what I wish always,
The lance of love for the joyous
That wounds the unprotected heart
With friendship's pleasant pleasing;
Yet I have felt such blow's assailing,
That from the deepest sleep I start.

Let her then show me mercy
And welcome, despite her grandeur,
Let me reveal the ill that pains me,
And how she adds to my dolour,
Into my heart now drives it further:
Love and sadness she grants to me,
For love of her, the best you'll see
From Le Puy down to Lleida.

Her rich worth is of the highest,
My lady they hold the noblest here,
Of all the world naked or dressed:
God made her gentle, to His honour,
She's chosen by the best wherever
She may choose to show her beauty,
And her true refined nobility
That with the best adorns her ever.

She is so noble, of sweet welcome,
I wish to take no other lover,
She's wise, mocks not at anyone,
With beauty blessed and with valour;
And not forgetting courtesy;
For usage of the courteous will
Protects her from all enmity still,
And every other infamy.

Note: *Lleida*, Lerida *in English until the 20th century, is one of the oldest towns in Catalonia.*

LO JORN QU'IE·US VI, DOMPNA, PRIMEIRAMEN,

The day I saw you, lady that first time,
When you were pleased to let me see,
All other thoughts departed from my mind,
And my wishes turned to you, utterly.
For, lady, you set desire in the heart
With one sweet smile, and a simple glance
Made me forget myself, all circumstance.

That great beauty and sweet conversation,
The noble speech and loving pleasure
That I knew there so dazed all sensation,
That to this hour, lady, I've not its measure.
Yours the concession, to plea of my true heart
That seeks to exalt your worth and honour;
Yours my submission, I could love no better.

And since I am so loyal to you, lady,
That Love grants me no power to love elsewhere,
But lets me pay court to one, maybe,
Who might remove the heavy grief I bear;
So when I think of you to whom joy bows,
All other love's forgotten and displaced:
With her my heart holds dearest, there it stays.

Remember, if you will, the promises,
You know you made me when we parted,
My heart then gay and filled with happiness,
Because sweet hope in me you commanded:
Great joy I felt then, now my ills increase,
Yet, when you please, I shall that joy know
Once more, sweet lady, for I live in hope.

And no ill treatment ever makes me dread,
Solely because I think my life will gain
From you, lady, some certain pleasure;
Whereby ills will be joy, delight again,
Solely through pain, for I know Love demands
That true lovers great wrongs still must pardon,
And for their good must bear an evil burden.

Ai! Lady, were this the hour when I might see
You, in your mercy, granting me such honour
By simply deigning then to call me lover!

ANC MAIS NO M·FO SEMBLAN

Never would I have conceived

That, for Love, my joy

And pleasure I would leave,

For sweetness tears employ:

Held in her power truly,

Love has me, for in me rise

Such sweet delights, I see

To serve her God made me

And for her worth I prize.

Often I have complained

Of her whom I do praise,

And then have thanked again

The root of my complaints,

And that's not strange, it's plain;

For those whom Love ennobles

Must suffer many things,

For often, the poet sings,

True good can conquer ills.

The lover can't complain
Nor confess to his harm,
Nor speak about his pain,
Nor praise the good, his balm,
If he seeks to change,
And is ever altering:
Many choose to talk
Knowing nothing of what
Brings joy or suffering.

None knows enough of love
To speak without trembling,
Yet I've seen laughter move,
Though not from joy arising,
And many the sighs that prove
No more than clever feigning;
Yet Love is leading me,
Towards the best I see,
Without shame or cheating.

Lady, the truest lovers
And the long-suffering too
And those that most flatter
Their lady and her truth,
Without orders, their ruler,
Through your courtliness
Will do what pleases you
And nothing I do rue,
Nothing but fears repress.

You so weigh on my mind
That when I pray I often
Think you are at hand,
Then your fresh complexion
Your body nobly planned,
So fill my memory
I think of nothing else,
And from this sweet thought well
Goodwill and courtesy.

'The poet and the four ladies'
Alain Chartier (b. 1385, d. c.1433)
Le Livre des Quatre Dames, c. 1425

BERTRAN DE BORN (C. 1140 - D. BEFORE 1215)

ertran de Born, a minor nobleman from the Limousin, shared with his brother the lordship of Autafort, or Altaforte, French: *Hautefort*, in the Périgord. One of the major troubadours of the twelfth century, his warlike nature and love of political intrigue, particularly his espousing the divisive cause of Henry, the Young English King, caused Dante to place him in the Inferno, Canto XXVIII, as a stirrer-up of strife. He ended his life as a monk in the abbey of Dalon, where his presence is recorded from 1197 to 1202.

"All this to make 'Una dompna soiseubuda', a borrowed lady, or as the Italians translated it 'Una donna ideale'"

— Ezra Pound

DOMPNA, PUOIS DE MI NO·US CAL

Lady, since you care not at all
For me, but keep me far from you,
And for no good reason too,
The task it seems immense
Of seeking some other,
Who might bring me new joy ever,
And if I have not the making
Of a lady as much to my liking,
Of the worth of she that's gone,
I shall love no other one.

Since I'll not find your equal,
Lovely as you, made as nobly,
Nor so joyous, sweet in body,
Lovely to every sense,
Nor so happy
Nor, by all repute, so worthy
I'll go seeking everywhere
A feature from each woman fair,
To make a borrowed lady
Till you look again toward me.

Colour fresh and natural
I'll take, fair Cembelins, from you
And your sweet love-glances too!
And risk the impertinence
Of forgoing there
All else in which you lack no share.
Then of Aelis I'll demand
Her adroit and charming tongue
Which must surely aid my suit,
That it be not dull or mute.

On Chalais' Vicomtess I call;
I'd have her give instantly
Her throat and hands to me.
Then take the journey thence,
Without straying,
To Rochechouart speeding
That Agnes her hair might grant me
Since Isolde, Tristan's lady,
Who was praised in every way
Was less fair than she today.

Audiart, though you wish me ill, in all,
I would that you dress her in your fashion,
That she might be well-adorned
And, as you are perfection, hence
Naught shall tear,
Nor love find aught improper.
Of my Lady Better-than-Best, my plea
Is her true fresh noble body
That shows her at first sight
Sweet to see naked if one might.

On the 'Exile', too I call
Wishing her white teeth, also
The welcome and conversation, so
Sweet in her presence
And her dwelling.
My 'Fair-Mirror' in your giving
Is your gaiety and stature
And what your fine manner
Displays, well-known as ever,
Never to change or waver.

My Lady, all I'd wish befall
Is that I might feel love, in truth,
For her as much as I do for you!
That a passionate intense
Love be sired,
One by my body well-desired,
Yet I'd rather of you demand
A kiss than any other woman,
So why does my love refuse me
When she knows I need her truly?

Papiol, straight to my Lover,
Go, for me now, sing to her,
That love's all disregarded, gone
From the heights, fallen headlong.

BE·M PLATZ LO GAIS TEMPS DE PASCOR

'And so that you may carry news of me, know that I am Bertrand de Born, he who gave evil counsel to the Young King. I made the father and the son rebel against each other'

– Dante: Inferno XXVIII, 134-136

The joyful springtime pleases me
That makes the leaves and flowers appear,
I'm pleased to hear the gaiety
Of birds, those echoes in the ear,
    Of song through greenery;
I'm pleased when I see the field
With tents and pavilions free,
    And joy then comes to me
All through the meadowlands to see
The heavy-armoured cavalry.

It pleases me when outriders
Make labourers and cattle flee,
It pleases me when follow after
Crowds of well-armed soldiery,
    And I am pleased at heart,
To see great castles forced by art
Their walls taken, rent apart,
    To see a host at war,
Enclosed by moats in every part,
With close-knit palisades and more.

I'm also pleased to view some lord
Who leads the vanguard in attack,
On armoured horse, a fearless sword,
Who can inspire his men to hack
    Away and bravely fight,
And when the conflict's joined aright,
Each must in readiness delight,
    And follow where he might,
For none attains to honour's height
Till blows have landed left and right.

Clubs and blades and painted helms
Shields that swords and lances batter
We'll see when fighting first begins,
And many vassals strike together,
    Their steeds will wander
Mounts of dead or wounded warrior;
And when he enters in the lather
    Let each noble brother,
Think only arms and heads to shatter,
Better to die than let them conquer.

It's not to my taste, I tell you,
Eating, drinking, sleeping, when
I hear voices cry: 'Set to!'
From either side, hearing then
    Horses neighing in the gloom,
And cries of 'Help me!', 'Aid me!' too,
And into the grassy ditch's tomb
    Fall great and small to their doom,
Seeing the corpses twice run through
By lances on which pennants loom.

Love would have lovers chivalrous,
Good with weapons, eager to serve,
Noble in language, generous,
Knowing how to act and observe
    Both outdoors and within,
According to the powers they're given.
Such as are pleasant company, then,
    Refined and courteous men.
She that in bed such love does win,
Is cleansed forever of her sin.

Noble Countess, you are the best
That's seen or ever will be seen,
Men say, compared with all the rest
The noblest lady on earth, I mean,
    High-born Beatrice,
Fine lady in acts and worthiness,
Fountain from which flows all goodness,
    And beauty all peerless,
Your rich fame is in such excess
Of all others you appear mistress.

    One of high lineage,
In whom is every beauty,
I love, am loved by her deeply;
    And she grants me courage,
So I'll not superseded be
By some other, presumptuously.

Barons, go pawn freely
All your castles, towns and cities,
Before ever you halt your armies.

Papiol, go swiftly
To Yea-and-Nay and gaily;
Say they're too long at peace.

Notes: *Yea-and-Nay is Richard I of England, younger brother of the Young English King, Henry.*

Papiol is Bertran de Born's court minstrel, jongleur *or* joglar.

'The siege'
Valerius Maximus, translated by Simon de Hesdin and
Nicholas de Gonesse
Les Fais et les Dis des Romains et de Autres Gens, pt 1,
c.1473 - c. 1480

AI! LEMOZIS, FRANCHA TERRA CORTESA,

Ah, Limousin! Country free and courtly,
I'm glad of this honour you receive,
Since joy and worth, repose and gaiety,
Courtesy, gallantry and sweet ease
Are come to us, may they never leave;
To serve her well we must quickly see
In what ways we might court this lady.

Gifts and tasks and ornaments freely
Aid love, as water fish in the sea,
Or as instruction, prowess, bravery,
Do courts, wars, tourneys, and weaponry;
Who claims both brave and skilled to be,
Does ill if he promises to deceive,
Since Lady Guiscarda's here directly.

Note: *Guiscarda was the wife of the Viscount of Comborn, and from Bourgogne. His friendship with her caused a rift between Bertran and Madonna Maent (Maeut de Montaignac, the wife of Talairan, brother of Talairan Count Elias V of Périgord 1166-1205. The name was later spelt Talleyrand!)*

GIRAUT DE BORNELH (C. 1138 – 1215)

iraut or Guiraut, also Borneil or Borneyll, was born to a lower class family in the Limousin, probably in Bourney, near Excideuil. Connected with the castle of the Viscount of Limoges, his skill earned him the nickname of Master of the Troubadours. He may have accompanied Richard I and Aimar V of Limoges on the Third Crusade. He certainly made a pilgrimage to the Holy Land but perhaps before the Crusade. His most famous poem is this *alba*, Reis glorios.

REIS GLORIOS, VERAIS LUMS E CLARTATZ,

Glorious king, true light and clarity,
Almighty God, Lord, in your charity,
Be a true help now to my friend!
For I've not seen him since day's end,
And soon it will be dawn.

Sweet friend, do you wake or are you sleeping?
Sleep no more, now, you must be waking!
For in the east I see a star rise
Day-bringer, star familiar to my eyes,
And soon it will be dawn.

Sweet friend, I sing now and I call to you!
Sleep no more: I hear the bird sing too
That goes to seek day in the greenery,
I fear you may be harmed by jealousy,
And soon it will be dawn.

Sweet friend, for me now go to the window
And gaze on the stars from earth below
And see how I am your true messenger!
If you will not, it is you will suffer,
And soon it will be dawn.

Fair friend, since I parted from
I've not slept, nor ceased praying too,
I pray to God, who's the son of Mary,
To give you to me in sweet loyalty,
And soon it will be dawn.

Fair friend, you begged me not to sleep
There at the threshold, but a true watch keep
On all through the night till it is day.
Now my song and presence you dismay,
Yet soon it will be dawn.

Fair friend, I am in so rich a way
I wish no more for the dawn of day,
For the noblest ever born of mother
I hold and embrace, so they're no matter
Not jealous fool or dawn.

PEIRE RAIMON DE TOULOUSE (FL. 1180 - 1220)

eire Raimon de Tolosa or Toloza was from the merchant class of Toulouse. He became a jongleur and spent time at the courts of Alfonso II of Aragon, William VIII of Montpellier, and probably, Raymond VI of Toulouse. He also lived in Italy (Lombardy and Piedmont), at the courts of Thomas I of Savoy, Guglielmo Malaspina, and Azzo VI of Este. Azzo's daughter Beatriz was the addressee of one of his poems. This poem of *fin'amor*, perfect or true love, is one of the more comprehensive statements of the troubadour ideal.

DE FIN'AMOR SON TOT MEI PENSAMEN

On true love are all my thoughts bent
And my desires and my sweetest days,
With true and faithful heart I'll serve always,
To live close to Amor I do consent,

And in simplicity I'll serve him still
Though my service bring me only ill,
Since they are painful and dangerous
The torments Love grants his followers.

Yet to me Love has such honour sent
Since my heart's firmer truer in its ways
Than any other man; and if it seldom says
Who it loves that's for fear of ill intent;

Should her sweet smile, face, eyes fail to tell,
And her fine and noble manners as well,
Her gaiety, and fair speech, miraculous,
Who she is to those who are connoisseurs!

And since your actions are so nobly meant
Humble, in trembling, my love I phrase,
For there is no lover as faithful always
As I to you, Lady, through this world's extent.

Through audacity, through pride I know full well
I sin, in loving you: often my eyes must fill,
With tears, for to direct my heart is ruinous
Towards one who is so high among the first.

Alas! A man cannot yearn and yet absent
Himself from where he'd most deeply gaze,
Or throw off sorrow and his spirits raise,
But swiftly seeks what his hope shall dent.

And know, lady, that the more my tears well,
The more love grows for you and my goodwill,
A sweet pleasant thought's born in my heart thus
Who, night and day, love's thoughts cannot disperse.

I dare to ask that your mercy, pity be lent
To one who finds no equal in these days,
To you; yet if one grants you service and aid,
Fair Lady, his own true gain is consequent.

And as you are, of all, most beautiful,
Most worthy, my service shall be more careful,
Than ever it was, no less continuous
The love for your dear honour I rehearse.

Sweet lady, I desire and want you still
More than the world, for true love draws
Me to the lovely body I praise in verse.

Refuge grants Rambertis de Buvalel,
To worth and merit, and so evermore
In joy and gaiety all here shall immerse.

ANONYMOUS AUBES (12TH - 13TH CENTURY)

QUAN LO ROSSINHOLS ESCRIA

While the nightingale sings away
To his mate both night and day
I'm with my sweet friend always,
Under the flower.
Till the watchman on the tower
Cries loudly: Lovers, now arise!

I see the dawn, and day's clear skies.

EN UN VERGIER SOTZ FUELLA D'ALBESPI

In a deep bower under a hawthorn-tree
The lady clings to her lover closely,
Till the watchman cries the dawn he sees,
Ah, God, Ah, God, the dawn! Is here so soon.

'Please God, now, night fail us not cruelly,
Nor my friend be parted far from me,
Nor day nor dawn, let the watchman see!
Ah, God, Ah, God, the dawn! Is here so soon.

Fine gentle friend, let us kiss, you and I,
Down in the meadow, where sweet birds sigh,
And all to each other, despite jealous eye.
Ah, God, Ah, God, the dawn! Is here so soon.

Fine gentle friend, we'll have sweet loving,
In the garden, where the small birds sing,
Till the watch his pipe sets echoing,
Ah, God, Ah, God, the dawn! Is here so soon.

Out of the sweet air that rises from my
Dear friend who's noble, handsome, and bright,
By his breath I'm touched, like a ray of light.'
Ah, God, Ah, God, the dawn! Is here so soon.

The lady's delightful and greatly pleases

Her beauty draws to her many gazes,

Yet in her heart love loyally blazes,

Ah, God, Ah, God, the dawn! Is here so soon.

Note: *The Occitan* caramehl, *the 'pipe' of verse four, is the 'chalumeau' in use in France from the twelfth century. The word refers to various sorts of pipes, some of which were made of cane and featured a single 'reed' cut into the side of the cane itself.*

'God the Father and angels'
Francisco de Ximenez, Livre des Anges, c. 1480

ANONYMOUS BALADE
(13TH CENTURY OR LATER)

MORT M'AN LI SEMBLAN QUE MADONA·M FAI

The glance that my lady darts at me must slay,
Born of her sweet eyes amorous and gay.

If I have none of her let me die alway;
The glance that my lady darts at me must slay.

On my knees I shall beg of her today;
The glance that my lady darts at me must slay.

Humbly before her then I go to pray,
That she solace me, one sweet kiss I'd weigh.

The glance that my lady darts at me must slay,
Born of her sweet eyes amorous and gay.

Her body's white as snow that on glacier lay,
The glance that my lady darts at me must slay.

Fresh is her colour as a rose in May,

The glance that my lady darts at me must slay.

Her hair, red gold, pleases in every way,

Softer and sweeter than a man can say.

The glance that my lady darts at me must slay,

Born of her sweet eyes amorous and gay.

God made none so beautiful nor may,

The glance that my lady darts at me must slay.

Her body I'll love, forever and a day,

The glance that my lady darts at me must slay.

And long as I live I'll not say her nay,

And die for her if I can't have my way.

The glance that my lady darts at me must slay,

Born of her sweet eyes amorous and gay.

Note: *Compare Chaucer's* 'Your eyen two whole slay me suddenly, I may the beauty of them not sustain. '

GAUCELM FAIDIT (C. 1170 – C. 1202)

orn in Uzerche, in the Limousin, from a family of knights in the service of the Count of Turenne, he travelled widely in France, Spain, and Hungary. His known patrons include Geoffrey II, Duke of Brittany and Dalfi d'Alvernha; he was at one time in Poitiers at the court of Richard I of England, on whose death he wrote this *planh*. It is possible, but controversial, that he took part in the Third Crusade from 1189-1191; it seems likely that in 1202 he set out on the Fourth Crusade, as did his then patron, Boniface of Montferrat. After 1202 there is no further mention of him.

FORTZ CHAUSA ES QUE TOT LO MAIOR DAN

A harsh thing it is that brings such harm,
The worst woe, alas, I've suffered: this!
Such that in weeping I will ever mourn,
For so I must sing it now, and utter,
That he the summit and crown of valour,
Noble, brave, Richard, King of the English,
Is dead! Ah, God! What harm, what loss!
What strange words, how grievous to hear!
Firm heart a man needs, that suffers here.

Dead is the king, and a thousand years gone
Since one of such worth was, such vile loss,
Nor was ever a man like him, not one,
So brave, so free, so generous, giving,
That none half as much or more has given,
Since Alexander thrashed Darius;
Not Charlemagne, nor Arthur, as valorous
As he who made men, if truth appear,
Either rejoice in him, or shake with fear.

I marvel that in this false world not one
Generous or courteous man should exist,
None now value good words, fine action,
And why should a man aim high or low?
Now Death has shown us his mighty blow,
Who at one stroke takes the best there is,
All honour, worth, oh, all good we miss;
Now he sees there is none to shield us,
A man may dread his own dying less.

Ai! Brave lordly king, what's to be done
With our vast armies, great tournaments,
Bright courts, and fine gifts and handsome,
If you're gone, that had their captaining?
What's to be done for those suffering,
All those for your good service meant,
Who waited on you, life's ornament?
What's to be done with them, in despair,
Whom you brought to great riches there?

A wretched life and worse death they'll win,

A grievous time, whether far or near;

And Saracen, Turk, Persian, Paynim,

Who, more than all, found you to dread,

Will grow in pride and power instead.

More slowly we'll gain the Sepulchre;

God wills so, for did he not, it's clear,

That if you, lord, had lived, unfailingly,

From Syria they'd have sought to flee.

No longer have I hope, through grace,

Some king or prince might all oversee;

For those who will occupy your place,

Needs have regard to their love of worth,

Your two brave brothers are under earth;

The Young King, noble Count Geoffrey,

And who remains to replace these three?

He'll need a lofty heart, firm thought,

To work good deeds, aid those he ought.

Ah, Lord God, You, our true pardoner,

True God: true man, true life, have mercy on

Him, who has pressing need of it, pardon,

And Lord, oh, look not on his error,

But how he served you, oh, now remember!

Note: *Richard I, the Lion Heart, was killed at the minor siege of Chalus-Chabrol in 1199, by a stray bolt from a crossbow. Of his two elder brothers, the Young King, Henry, had died in 1183, and Geoffrey, Duke of Brittany, in 1186. His younger brother John succeeded him as king.*

'Charlemagne'
Renaut de Montauban (or Les Quatre Fils Aimon)
Second quarter of the 15th century

PEIRE CARDENAL (C. 1180 – C. 1278)

eire Cardenal, or Cardinal was born in Le Puy-en-Velay educated as a canon, but abandoned his career in the church for 'the vanity of this world' according to his *vida*. He began his career at the court of Raymond VI of Toulouse and subsequently travelled widely, visiting the court of James I of Aragon. He died at an advanced age in Montpellier.

VERA VERGENA MARIA

Truest Virgin, our Maria

True of life, and true of faith,

True in truth, and our truth clear,

True in virtue, the true way,

Truest friend, truest mother,

True in love, true mercy's ray,

Through true mercy now declare

Among your heirs I'll be one day.

Lady, grant this, if you please,

That from your son to us flow Peace.

You repair for us the folly
That saw Adam overcome;
You, the star, guiding gently
Pilgrims passing through our land;
You then are the Dawn of day
To which the son of God is Sun,
Shining warmly, shining brightly,
Of true righteousness the sum.

Lady, grant this, if you please,
That from your son to us flow Peace.

You were born in Syria,
Gentle, poor in worldly goods;
Ever humble, pious, purer,
In all done, said, understood,
Fashioned by such a Master,
Without all evil, with all good,
Of such sweet company there
That in you was harboured God.

Lady, grant this, if you please,
That from your son to us flow Peace.

194

He, who in you puts his trust,
Needs no other for defence,
Such that if the world were lost
He will not be carried hence;
Before your worth, the mightiest
Is humbled, if the man has sense,
And your son will not protest
At your wish, takes no offence.

Lady, grant this, if you please,
That from your son to us flow Peace.

David in his prophecies
Says, in a psalm of old,
That at God's right hand will be,
Near the King that law foretold,
A Queen who in finery
Will be dressed, in vair and gold.
Without fail you are she,
No plea to you can be too bold.

Lady, grant this, if you please,
That from your son to us flow Peace.

'Virgin and Child'
Book of Hours, first quarter of the 15th century

SORDELLO (FL. 1220 - 1265)

ordello da Goito or Sordel de Goit, sometimes *Sordell*, was born in the municipality of Goito in the province of Mantua. Praised by Dante in the *De vulgari eloquentia*, he is, in the *Purgatorio* of *The Divine Comedy*, made the type of patriotic pride, bemoaning the state of Italy, as partially substantiated by the *planh* below. In 1226, while at the court of Richard of Bonifazio in Verona, he abducted his master's wife, Cunizza, at the instigation of her brother, Ezzelino da Romano. The scandal resulted in his flight (1229) to Provençe. He entered the service of Charles of Anjou, and probably accompanied him (1265) on his Naples expedition; in 1266 he was a prisoner in Naples. The last documentary mention of him is in 1269, and he is supposed to have died in Provençe.

'....and the spirit all pre-occupied with self, surged towards him from the place where it first was, saying: 'O Mantuan, I am Sordello, of your city.'

— Dante: Purgatorio VI:72-75

PLANHER VUELH EN BLACATZ EN AQUEST LEUGIER SO

I wish to mourn Blacatz, now, in skilful song,
With dark, grieving heart, and mortal reason,
Since I lose in him so noble, fair a companion,
And all his worthiness swift to death is gone;
Now I've no hope at all, so mortal the harm,
Of any remedy, no ounce of hope, not one;
Rend his heart: let these barons eat it to a man,
Those without heart since from it heart is won.

Let the Emperor of Rome, who has most need,
Eat first of the heart, if he'd take the Milanese
By force of conquest, they checked him indeed,
He's disinherited, despite his German breed;
Then let the King of France be the next to eat:
And win that Castile he did so rashly cede;
Yet let him not, if his mother be displeased,
For he'll do nothing now, if *she*'s not agreed.

The King of England too, who lacks all valour,
I'd wish to see him eat, gain courage, power,
So that land he dishonoured, he may recover,
Taken by France's King, who knows his blather.
Let Castile's King eat for himself, and another,
Of two kingdoms, king, and yet worth neither;
If he eats, let him do so beneath the cover,
If he's found out, he'll be beaten, by *his* mother.

Aragon's King, I would that he'd do the same,
Since by so doing he'd free himself from shame,
Who suffers Marseille, Millau; his mortal fame
Wins him no honour, for all he may do or claim.
I'd have the King of Navarre eat then, in name
A king though more a count, so dull his game.
What grief when God seeks to glorify the lame,
Those that lack heart and prove but weak and tame.

The Count of Toulouse, as well, must eat and how,
Knowing what he had, knowing what he has now,
If a second heart can't help his cause somehow,
His own won't help him win what's lost, I trow.
The Count of Provençe must eat the last, allow
That, disinherited, he's not worth a sow,
Despite how he yet defends himself, I vow
He'll eat the heart, to bear what makes him bow.

For my song, the barons wish me ill, truly,
Yet know I'll value them as they value me.

Bel Restaur, if I only have your mercy,
I scorn men for whom I prove ill company.

Notes: *Blacatz, Blacas de Blacas III (1165-1237), was feudal lord of Aups and a troubadour.*

The Roman Emperor is Frederick II of Sicily. The King of France is Louis IX. The King of Castile is Ferdinand III of Castile and Léon. The King of England is Henry III. The King of Aragon is James I, cousin of Count Raymond Bérenger IV. The King of Navarre is Thibaut IV of Champagne, the poet king. The Count of Toulouse is Raymond VII. The Count of Provence is Raymond Bérenger.

Amilau, or Millau in Aveyron, on the banks of the Tarn, was the major source of earthenware in the Roman Empire, and site of one of the major bridges over the Tarn. Subject to the King of Aragon from 1172, it was taken by Raymond VI of Toulouse in 1222, and James I of Aragon finally ceded his rights to the town in 1258 to France. Marseille which established itself as a republic during the period was at the centre of conflict for decades. In 1246 it finally passed to Charles of Anjou, Count of Provence.

Bel Restaur, 'the lovely one who restores me', or the Fair Healer, may be Guida da Rodez, 1212-1265, daughter of Henri I Count of Rodez. She married Pons VI of Montlaur in 1226. She was then Baronne de Posquières, de Castries et de Montlaur, and became a patroness of troubadours.

AI LAS E QUE-M FAN MEI UEHLS

Alas, what use are my eyes
If they see not what I prize?

Though summer renew and adorn
Itself with leaf and flower
Yet however I sing and mourn,
She, the lady of pleasure,
Cares not for my prayers forlorn,
I'll sing, I'll die a lover,
So loving her, dusk to dawn,
For little do I see her.

Alas, what use are my eyes
If they see not what I prize?

Although love cause me to sigh,
I'll not complain of a thing;
For the noblest, I choose to die,
Though evil for good may sting,
So long as she consents that I
Hope, mercy she yet may bring,
Whatever suffering I may buy,
I'll not claim for anything.

Alas, what use are my eyes
If they see not what I prize?

I die if her love she'll not give,
For I cannot see or dream
Where I can turn or how I'll live,
If she so distant seem,
No other could please I believe,
Nor make me forget, I deem;
Whatever the love I conceive
The more Love shall I esteem.

Alas, what use are my eyes
If they see not what I prize?

Ah, why does she treat me harshly?
She knows how it comforts me,
To sing, and praise one so worthy,
I'm hers, the more painfully
She exalts or abases me,
I can't prevent it, truly,
Far from her I'd not wish to be,
Though living death is my fee.

Alas, what use are my eyes
If they see not what I prize?

So I'll beg my sweet friend in song,
Please don't kill me, sinfully.
If she knows it to be a wrong
When I'm dead she'll grieve for me,
Yet I'd rather she brought death on,
Than live as her pleasure decree,
Worse than death not to see the one
Whom I love so tenderly.

Alas, what use are my eyes
If they see not what I prize?

GUIRAUT RIQUIER (C. 1230 - 1292)

ne of the last, if not the last, of the true Provençal troubadours, Guiraut survived the Albigensian Crusade and the wars that effectively destroyed the cultured society that had supported them. He served Aimery IV, Viscount of Narbonne, as well as Alfonso el Sabio, King of Castile. He is also believed to have served Henry II, Count of Rodez. He made this somewhat ironic *alba* in 1257, a fitting coda to the troubadour era.

AB PLAZEN

From pleasant

Thoughts now and

Amorous,

Sufferings call

Despite all

Carefulness,

I sleep not though I tire,

So toss, and turn, and gyre,

    And desire

      To see the dawn.

From such gales

Pain assails

Day and night,

Joy now fails

So prevails

Sad heart's plight,

So at night fiercer fire

Consumes my mind entire,

     And desire

     To see the dawn.

Sad awake

Till daybreak

Watch I keep,

No pleasure

To lie there

Without sleep,

Joyless love deep in the mire;

So that with sighs I respire,

     And desire

     To see the dawn.

Bringing harm

Night wears on,

It would seem.

Such chagrin

I've not known

No sweet dream,

For I can't see her I admire,

Though to comfort her I aspire,

    And desire

      To see the dawn.

'God creating the sun and moon'
Guyart des Moulins, Bible historiale, c. 1420

About the Translator

nthony Kline lives in England. He graduated in Mathematics from the University of Manchester, and was Chief Information Officer (Systems Director) of a large UK Company, before dedicating himself to his literary work and interests. He was born in 1947. His work consists of translations of poetry; critical works, biographical history with poetry as a central theme; and his own original poetry. He has translated into English from Latin, Ancient Greek, Classical Chinese and the European languages. He also maintains a deep interest in developments in Mathematics and the Sciences.

He continues to write predominantly for the Internet, making all works available in download format, with an added focus on the rapidly developing area of electronic books. His most extensive works are complete translations of Ovid's Metamorphoses and Dante's Divine Comedy.

Made in United States
North Haven, CT
17 March 2022

17243467R00117